Distance Education and Curriculum Organisation

Implications for Language Teaching

Jaya Vuppala

Foreword by
V.C. Kulandaiswamy

1995

Kaveri Books
Delhi - 110085.

ISBN 81-7479-005-5

Published by : Rakesh Goel
Kaveri Books
125, Kadambari, 19/IX, Rohini
Delhi - 110085 (India)
Phone: 7265687

Laser Typeset by : ShiKi Associates, New Delhi.

Printed at : Raj Offset Works, Delhi.

PRINTED IN INDIA

In the Loving Memory of
My Father

Late Shri N. Lakshmayya

Foreword

If Distance Education is picking up as a new system elsewhere, in India it is gradually assuming the dimensions of a revolution in education. When the urge for democratic polity and a more humane civil society grow stronger, the demand for equal opportunities for all to go for quality education upto the highest level is made all the more emphatically. The inherent weaknesses in terms of resources—both material and human—that plague the less developed countries should be countered with new strategies to achieve the desired goal with the available resources. Taking into account the range of constraints starting from shortage of funds to lack of human resources of acceptable academic standards, one must think of a viable alternative strategy and a realistic agenda for freeing education from the clutches of stifling restrictions and fossilised ideas about education as such. As a strategy, distance education fullfils the demand. But the implementation of it in a realistic and workable way depends on a number of prerequisites.

Outside the political context, distance education draws much of its strength from technology, particularly from the multimedia. Granting the availability of technology and the multimedia, the availability of the right kind of human material is the most important prerequisite in making the distance education system work. Mechanical and stereotype activities of individuals may be alright in a factory-like situation and in the process of mechanical reproduction of ideas and culture. But, then, even the production of goods and commodities in constantly under compulsion to go in for innovation and new strategies of planning, managing and marketing because of the pressure of competition and survival. Education being a part of the 'super-structure', it too gets influenced by the tremors of the 'structure' or the economic base. However, when the policy makers and the practitioners of education operate at the realm of ideas within the educational subsystem with relative autonomy, they have to think more seriously about the need or innovation, novelty and social relevance of academic inputs. Such a need is felt nowhere more intensely than in the area of curriculum.

Unfortunately, till today there has been no significant advance made in curriculum planning and development worth its name either at the national level or at the State level. There is no holistic approach to curricular issues, and to whatever syllabi that have been used hitherto; they are conceived on the basis of routine practices rather than on a sound philosophical or scientific basis. Since curriculum is the base on which the academic edifice must be built, it is necessary that policy makers and academicians given it the importance it really deserves. This issue assumes more importance in the context of distance education.

Distance education has the potential to reach those sections of the population who have not so far been able to have access to education because of various constraints. More importantly it has the flexibility to offer and accommodate a range of unconventional, innovative courses and instructional methods and delivery mechanisms. Any distance education programme therefore needs to be carefully considered at the stage of developing and designing the basic curriculum. Traditionally, curriculum has been framed from the point of view of pedagogy, i.e., from the teacher's point of view. Distance education moves away from this position in favour of androgogical principles and allows considerable freedom for the learner autonomy to unfold itself-of course, with the necessary support from the educational institution. Those who have the responsibility to develop the new curricula will have to think in terms, not only of novelty of content but also of the new approaches to the philosophy of education. Progressive ideas and concepts regarding new curricula will have a definite bearing on the practice of distance education.

Jaya Vuppala has made a very useful contribution through her consideration of the educational ideas of some of the radical thinkers such as Knowles, Freire, Rogers, Paterson, Piaget, Bruner, Vygotsky, Dewey, Illich, Gelpi and others. She has also pointed out the implications of the alternative form of curriculum as outlined by her for language teaching. She has brought out two important aspects very well: the viability of considering new form of curriculum through distance mode, and the necessity to link it to language teaching–in this case the teaching of English. Both the aspects need to be discussed further, and widening of the horizon of new curriculum is possible only through such discussions and debates. The present work is a good starting point in that direction. It is certainly a valuable addition to the literature on the subject. The author and the publisher deserve to be congratulated for the contribution made to distance education on an important subject field.

I hope and trust that planners and policy makers in education as well as academics would welcome and encourage this commendable effort

Ex. Vice Chancellor **V.C. Kulandaiswamy**
I.G.N.O.U.,
Maidan Garhi,
New Delhi 110 068.

Preface

A distance mode of education will gain in relevance to meet the awareness and educational needs of developing countries in the period ahead. While it will not replace the face-to-face, class room instruction it could increasingly supplement the conventional mode especially to reach the remote areas and to provide access to socio-economically less privileged groups for equalising their chances of benefiting from higher education.

Ms. Jaya Vuppala in her study speaks for an alternative curriculum to replace the traditional educational discrimination resultant in the conventional mode especially for language teaching. In school atmosphere perpetuates class distinction in favour of the upper class whereas correspondence and media based, distance mode democratizes information and it serves as a supplementary relationship to learning and language development. Her analysis of correspondence theory of education as reflexive is appropriate for language learning.

More about the politics of education and educational theory, the argument of Ms. Jaya Vuppala's book raises meaningful questions about the social construction of reality, subject formation and the institutionalisation of knowledge. An attempt, worthwhile and well-taken, has been made to discuss clearly in a logical sequence of steps the manner in which 'pedagogy' should be distinguished from 'androgogy' while offering a scholarly analysis of the primary and secondary sources, from Piaget to Illich and Friere. The conclusions arrived at, and the caution offered at the end, are carefully derived from a mature appreciation of the 'problematics' of adult education in general, and distance education in particular.

Ms. Jaya Vuppala does make a significant contribution to existing theoretical knowledge about adult education. Although she appears to devote a greater amount of attention to theory, the implications relevant to 'curriculum organisation' and to 'language learning' clearly follow from the analysis. The discussion ranges from an analysis of the progressive paradigm in education and language learning which is mainly psychology-oriented to a sociology-oriented account of the environment and cultural relations which are deeply connected with curriculum organisation. There is commendable clarity of purpose when she offers a critique of the correspondence theory of education as also the phenomenological theory where reflexivity counts.

The methodology of distance education, she urges rightly, should constantly strive to be "learner-friendly" avoiding the perils of dehumanisation. Equality of opportunity may prove to be an elusive social goal but equal access to educational opportunity, she observes, should be a reality with the correct use of the distance education mode.

The argument of the book would gain in relevance and value if primary data about learners and material available with an institution like the Dr. B R Ambedkar Open University is applied and examined in relation to curriculum design and delivery. Thus the distance could be closed through constant monitoring of feedback for course correction.

This work is of seminal relevance to those engaged in teaching and research in general and language learning in particular through the distance education mode. I strongly commend her work to all those seeking alternative modes of learning, teaching extension and evaluation.

Vice-Chancellor, **S. Bashiruddin**
Dr. B.R. Ambedkar Open University,
Hyderabad-500 482.

Acknowledgements

I am grateful to Dr. Lalitha Eapen for her guidance and encouragement in the preparation of the manuscript. I am also grateful to Prof. Kulandaiswamy for his valuable foreword. I am also grateful to Prof. Basheeruddin for his thoughtful comments in his preface.

I am grateful to Babu, my husband, for the inspiration and support he provided, during the project. I am also thankful to my father Late Shri N. Lakshmayya, my mother Smt. Sita Devi, and my sister Vijaya, for helping me concentrate on my work, through accepting some of my domestic responsibilities.

I also acknowledge the help extended by my children Rishi and Dingu, in leaving me alone at the right times.

Finally, I am grateful to the effort put in by the ITC staff, who include Uma, Vishi and Magesh in the preparation of this document.

Lastly, I acknowledge my own effort in attempting to write this manuscript, after a gap of nearly a decade, in the true spirit of Distance Education.

Jaya Vuppala

Acknowledgements

[illegible]

Contents

Glossary

Androgogy	Pertains to adult learning. The term coined by Knowles, emphasises adult learning as opposed to child learning, by focussing on adult characteristics.
Autonomous	The quality of a mature self directed adult. With reference to education, the autonomous student is one who can manage his/her learning and evaluate, without seeking help from the teacher or others.
Banking Concept	Freire's term for the belief predominant over the years that the student is an ignorant empty vessel which has to be filled with information from the knowledge bank, who is the teacher.
Behaviourist	A scientific paradigm deriving from Skinner's theory. The Skinnerian experiment based on the stimulus response duality proved that when a stimulus produced an agreeable response was rewarded, it became a habit. If the stimulus produced a negative response, it could be discouraged by a negative reward.
Correspondence	The strong assumption that most Marxists held that the School structures correspond to those of the society at

	large with similar divisions and inequalities.
Egalitarian	An institution or individual that believes in equality of opportunity.
Habitualisation	Activities which get routinised by sheer repetition day after day, become as mechanical as habits. Socialisation begins with habits.
Humanists	As a reaction against the behaviourists (which reduced the human entity by treating him on par with the animals) came a wave of humanism. Predominantly, in education the aim was to make every allowance to regain the lost glory of the human.
Institutionalisation	A particular set of activities pertaining to an occupation or a social group get routinised to an extent that they do not change.
Learner-centred	Refers to a curriculum which gives ample scope to the learner, in terms of initiative, motivation ands also allows for pacing depending on the learner capability.
Pedagogy	The art of teaching a child. Traditionally, no difference was made between teaching a child and an adult, within the educational framework.
Phenomenological	A philosophical stance where the individual subjectivity is given utmost significance. Therefore,truth ,is only a notion, a relative notion, that differs from individual to individual and from perception

	to perception. This relativity makes for a curriculum that is basically flexible and defies an absolute meaning.
Process syllabus	A syllabus that emerges from the class as a result of interactive negotiation among its participants. In this sense, its a syllabus in retrospect is a methodological innovation that is a fusion of both content and form.
Progressive	A paradigm position which celebrates individual freedom as opposed to all controls both state and institutional. Implications for individual learning and curriculum design extend from this basic stance.
Reflexive curriculum	A curriculum can be said to be reflexive to the extent it makes allowance for varied interpretations and refuses to be seen as a top down artifact.
Streaming	A process of selection whereby two different groups are made,the elite and the non-elite, with a different curriculum designed for each of these groups.

Introduction

The book attempts to make a critical study of Distance Education as an alternative form of curriculum organisation with specific reference to language teaching and learning. It sets out to explore the possibilities of the distance education, as far as the language Curriculum is concerned, keeping in mind, the major themes along which it operates. Distance Systems basically cater to an adult, working, autonomous learner, set within a curricular framework geared to the average learner. Unlike the traditional face to face Curriculum then, aspects that focus on the learner, such as the self-directed learning, and the distance that separates the learner from the teacher or the educational institution call for a re-organisation that is of positive advantage to the learner.

In Curriculum organisation, this focus on the learner that the Progressive stance takes, asks for a re-appraisal in the light of the claims of Distance Education *as learner centered.* Therefore, as a take-off point, the first chapter discusses the Progressive stance in pedagogy and the importance this has for language education. This Progressive stance has been discussed at length because as mentioned earlier, (1) it deals with the individual which is the primary concern of Distance Education. (ii) It deals with the work of developmental psychologists like Piaget and educationists like Dewey and Bruner, who are primarily dealing with the Curriculum. Curriculum, a learner centered one, like distance education being the major concern for us, the attempt is to study the

Curriculum organisation as it relates to the individual in terms of the positive aspects it hold for the learner. Distance Education Curriculum being at a distance from the learner, can only hold credibility in so far as it cuts down this distance and help learning take place.

Chapter One explores Curriculum in traditional terms before applying it to a large geographical and spatial set up like Distance Education. Here the Progressive version of language Curriculum is first discussed.

This Chapter on 'Pedagogy' is basically divided into two sections

(i) Where the Progressive philosophy is discussed for the importance it gives to the learner, in terms of capabilities to work out for oneself, with a given sufficient amount of support. Basically, as the Progressivists see it, the school helps in this function.

(ii) Where it deals with the specific curricula arrangements, these are proposed to activate and help the learner become autonomous.

Process Syllabuses, the Progressivists like Breen and Candlin claim, are ideal for promoting language acquisition. These interactive setups, they feel are ideal for language learning processes to function. The Chapter concludes on the limitation of the pedagogical set up, the Progressivists project by identifying (i) The idealistic frame, in which the Piagetian studies make sense. (ii) The social vacum in which the learner is posited.

Chapter Two explores the Curriculum issues, and implications for language, emerging from the traditional framework, as they now relate to Androgogy or the adult learning set up. In so far as a distinction was made, this has been purely on a psychological basis. This is of course crucial to Distance Education as it has to come to terms with the adults, their psychological capacity to learn a language, and the strategies that they use in attempting to learn. This Chapter discusses the arguments of Knowles, Paterson and other important writers for their emphasis on adult characteristics in learning. This Chapter is again basically divided into two sections:

(i) Dealing with the theoretical discussions of major writers concerned with adult learning and

(ii) Dealing with the specific psychic abilities that the adult is endowed with for acquiring/learning a language. Both these aspects are crucial for the Distance Mode, geared as it is to the adult and the motivation that it has to maintain to see that the student does not drop out. This is significant in so far as the Distance Mode has to operate without the constant interaction with the teacher, and also the fact that the learner is left to his her own resources, at times when motivation is low.

The Chapter concludes by focussing on the limitation of the Progressive stance in describing adulthood as unproblematic. In dealing with the Distance Mode the Chapter asserts, it is necessary to move beyond the asocial and apolitical concept of the adult and locate the individual adult-learner in a given socio-economic stratum.

Chapter Three then attempts to redefine the crucial issues as regards the learner, autonomy, Curriculum and the basic assumptions that one has to grapple with, when one deals with the Distance System of education. The Chapter begins by exploring one particular trend in sociology that deals with the Correspondence Principle. Both within the pedagogical and the androgogical set up, this '*correspondence*' is visible in the repression and elimination of the lower class individual and the glorification of the upper class individual.

Particular emphasis is given to the works of Apple and Bowles and Gintis, especially their early work where the correspondence principle is emphasized. However, of their own admission such '*correspondence*' essentially gives a narrow picture. The school, they note, has a potential for change. This is visible through the contradictions it presents. The Chapter concludes on the positive implications and the wider scope for change that such contradictions bring forth.

Chapter Four describes concrete manifestations of the correspondence principle through asserting the existence of two different streams of education (i) Meant for the Upper Class, (ii) Meant for the Lower Class. The Chapter explores historically, the maintaining of distinctions between the two streams, as also the controversy on establishing a common core Curriculum. From this context, it locates Distance Education as a form of education that should be looked on as an *alternative* form of Curriculum organization, and not an alternative to the existing lower stream curricula.

In so far as Distance claims to serve the under-privileged, further streaming would only replace one kind of Curriculum for another without significantly changing the *low status* given to the lower stream. Therefore, it is argued, that Curriculum in the Distance Mode should make it possible to posit a primary Curriculum in which certain skills can be best taught through the Distance Mode and others through the face to face contact. The basis of streaming then applies not to individual learners but to the skills that have to be taught.

Chapter Five broadens the scope of the sociological analysis in directions indicative of movements beyond the correspondence. These have positive implications for the Distance Mode. It explores the various trends in sociology including the positivist and the phenomenological. Of the two, the phenomenological, it is asserted, suggests the *alternate 'possibilities'* that are of particular significance to the Distance Mode of Education. The Chapter explores crucial issues related to knowledge as the selection, distribution and evaluation of a particular kind of knowledge which is termed high status as against others which are rated low. By framing these issues as also those which relate to the nature of the investigation involved, it also indicates the possibility of multiple perspectives and opens the way for other meanings to take over.

Chapter Six looks at Distance Education as precisely the alternate meaning; an alternate organisation of Curriculum which disregards traditional notions of discrimination. It examines the notions of the autonomous learner as also the openness that makes this alternate organisation possible. In this altered context, with the distinct socio-economic definition, it is suggested that the Process elements that the Progressivists project have better options to become functional, operable. For here is a context, which is true, and therefore due consideration is given to the handicaps, (*presented as non-existent in the Progressive stance*) with which the learner has to function.

The book concludes on a note of caution. It warns against the possibility of this '*alternate curriculum*' becoming yet another basis for bypassing the disadvantaged learner; this time through legitimating the procedures of implementation. This, it is argued, is a distinct possibility if Distance Education is projected as a substitute curriculum for the disadvantaged learner. Further, the economical benefit that Distance Education ensures, might play into the hands of the technocrat, who might then use it as an area for investment for purely commercial purposes. That is precisely why Distance Education is here referred to as an alternative form of curriculum organisation and not as another curriculum for the low stream education.

1

Pedagogy

Traditionally, Pedagogy was considered equivalent to education, irrespective of whether the learner concerned was a child or an adult. Therefore, what applied to the child was regarded as applicable to all learners and the learning situation in general. The focus in this Chapter is primarily on Pedagogy as it applies to all learning, the Progressive pedagogy to highlight the importance that the Progressivists give to the individual learner. Our concern with Distance Education is similarly related to this focus on the individual learner. The attempt is, therefore, to try and see whether this predominant Progressive concern with the individual has similarities to the individual learner as conceived in the distance education mode. This Chapter is really a take off point for further exploration in this direction.

Developmental Psychologists like Piaget and educational psychologists like Bruner and Dewey have been concerned with the individual and his/her development. Basically dealing with psychological perspectives, these writers have made significant contributions to the curriculum with which we are directly concerned. That their main focus has been the individual learner within this curriculum set up is of special significance for the distance mode. The Process elements that the Progressivists uphold are promises that the Distance Mode can well profit from. Despite the fact that these *processes* occur within the classroom set up, it is not difficult to comprehend the potential possibilities for the Distance Mode.

In-so-far as the Process elements basically revolve round the individual learner, they have crucial significance for the Distance Mode, which necessarily has its main focus on the learner, left to himself/herself. Aspects such as acknowledging the learner's point of view, interacting with the material at hand, and so on have important implications for the Distance Mode. Within the framework of language learning and teaching, such elements are crucial for curriculum formulations. This is precisely why the 'Progressive' point of view and the implications it has for curriculum is discussed in this chapter.

A Historical Perspective

One of the most distressing features of the behaviourist psychology was its tendency to impose on human, the results it found in experimentation with rats and rabbits. As if in revolt, Chomskian studies set the trend for an increasingly human domain. Significantly so in language research, which it was asserted as unquestionably species-specific. In his footsteps were the humanists who sought tirelessly to restore to humanity all that it lost in the behaviourist hands. With the toppling of the behaviourist modalities, it seemed as if no effort was lost in using all forces to reinstate the human glory.

Important educationists including Carl Rogers (1983) spoke of education as self-realization. For Rogers, the environment of learning is one where pain, pleasure and frustration are freely expressed. For, learning is learning about one's self. Learner potential, for Rogers, needs to be captured at all moments. So the learner needs of necessity be free; free to choose, free to talk, free to express his/her frustration. Only then true learning occurs. Similarly, for Malcom Knowles (1983), who mainly speaks of the adult learner, the freedom to learn what one chooses and the pace at which the learner conveniently do so, call for an autonomy, which was in the behaviourist framework, a virtual taboo.

This humanistic sweep had significant pedagogical implications. Traditionally, the educational framework was controlled by the teacher who was the model for the learner. Within the limits of the classroom, is was virtually a teacher-centered class, with the material being organised at the discretion of the teacher or the syllabus designers. The learner, in other words, was posited at the zero level of cognition. In Frerian (1983) terms, the *Banking Concept* was the trend of education. Such a format, however, came into a lot of criticism both from educationists and psychologists in the wake of the Chomskian insights, and the humanistic invasion that followed.

The Progressive Viewpoint

According to the theories of cognitive development as elaborated by Piaget (1976), Bruner (1975) and Vygotsky (1986), there is nothing like the zero level of cognition. Individual children are seen as active participants in the process of learning right from infancy. Much of the research within the humanistic tradition that held sway in the Post-Chomskian era focussed on the influence of language on one or the other cognitive processes. Interest has centered particularly on how language shaped thought. The emphasis is on language universals and how they impart a universally human character to all information processing whatever the culture. The concept of psychic unity of mankind, says Bruner (1975), has replaced the doctrine of cultural relativism.

Language seems to have a profound effect on the mental processes, especially in contexts which are not immediate. Most psychologists are now agreed that there are norms of thought which are non-verbal but that, without language, thinking is limited. While Chomsky's innateness theory claimed the universally present LAD (Language

Acquisition Device), it seemed to underplay the environmental factors which became crucial for developmental psychologists like Piaget, Bruner and even more significantly for Vygotsky. It is in this interaction with environment that language is processed and leads to cognitive development. It is in this context that the school as an educational context becomes significant. We shall discuss significant contributions of these major thinkers.

Piaget

In the Piagetian cosmos, each child is invested with an intelligence that grows and develops by the actions that he/she performs on objects, in his/her own time. This intellectual capacity is changing, evolving, growing stage upon stage, so that adult thinking is not the same as child thinking, though it grows out of child thinking. According to Piaget this intelligence in children as in adults grows out of co-operative exchange between the child and his environment, which includes the adults. To understand Piaget, Sarah Campbell (1976) asserts that it is necessary to substitute for notions of norm, IQ and competition, equally valid notions of individuality, universal intelligence and co-operation, where the individual child has peculiarities of his own, while sharing an intelligence that is universal, and always in interaction or co-operation with the environment. Of particular importance in the Piagetian Experiment has been the essential pre-occupation with the analysis of those complex structures of thought that characterize the various developmental stages. Elaborating on one of these structures namely reversibility, Piaget observes that "intelligence is above all characterized by operations that are reversible actions".

Distinguishing these reversible operations from habits, Piaget observes that habits are not reversible, they are oriented in one direction only. To reverse the habit requires the learning of a new habit. By contrast, to solve a problem is to co-ordinate operations by focussing on the solution. Operations, as Piaget defines them, are actions which are reversible. This is very obvious when dealing with a mathematical problem. The learner can work it one way, in one direction, and also the other way in the opposite direction. According to Piaget, this concept of reversibility cannot be understood, until children are at a certain age, when their thinking becomes capable of reversible operations and when such operations become co-ordinated structures.

Piaget traces four stages in the development of this reversibility.

1. The pre-language sensori-motor stage.
2. The pre-operational stage.
3. The stage of concrete operations.
4. The stage of propositional operations.

Sensori Motor Stage

During the Sensori motor stage, the child develops sub-structures essential for later operation. It is generally acknowledged now that the pre-lingual child has intelligence. This intelligence constructs invariants that relate to the permanency of the object, in so far as it occupies the concrete space of immediate action.

The infant is not capable of attributing a permanency to the object that exists outside his perceptual field. When the object is taken away from his field of vision he loses interest in it. Later on he begins to look for the missing object. The disappearance of the object elicits search and the search is guided by observed displacements. These displacements imply the possibility of movement in one direction and in the reverse by which the object can be reached over an alternate variety of patternings.

Pre Operational Stage

This stage heralds the development of representational thinking, often observed in the imaginary games the children play. In these games one thing comes to be represented by another, as when children imitate others. Such representational thinking widens the range of intellectual activity, which no longer confines itself to the immediate space. The child must now construct on an ideational plane the invariants and the forms of co-ordination whose beginnings were observed in the sensori motor stage. This stage marks the beginning of language. During this period both thought and representation develop but not the logical operations defined as interiorized reversible action systems. Visual correspondence is crucial at this stage. Thus in the Piagetian example of conservation the conclusions are based on the gross perceptual configuration which is different when the same quantity of liquid is poured into a high beaker.

The child at this stage proceeds by three arguments. The first which Piaget terms the identity arguments suggests, that since nothing has been added or taken away, the quantity is the same.

The second argument provides a reason. The reason according to the child is that on reversing the process, that is by pouring the content back into the original container, it will look the same. Identity is the product of the original operation and its reversal.

The third argument is again based on a kind of reversibility but in the form of a pattern of a relationship. These multiple relationships that the child traces in the simple operation relate to the variations in height, width and so on.

Formal Operation Stage

Here the adolescent is no longer limited to concrete reasoning about objects, he begins to do so hypothetically.

At this stage the adolescent can start from a theoretical assumption and reason out if it is true. This hypothetico-deductive method presupposes implication, disjunction, compatibility, operations characteristic of the logic of propositions. The child first discovers proportions through experience, for instance, as he finds out that adding weight on a balance produces the same result as increasing a constant weights distance from the fulcrum and vice versa. In this way he learns the equivalence of two transformations. At the same time the child discovers reciprocal relationships that is, if he increases the weight he must decrease the distance, if he increases distance he must decrease weight to maintain equilibrium.

The child expresses all these relationships in simple everyday language but his language describes his reasoning exactly. The child can now state that increasing the weight while decreasing the distance gives the same result as decreasing the weight and increasing distance. There is thus, a restructuring of the concrete operations so that the new operations can be constituted as second order operations integrating the earlier one. Therefore, starting from a stage where the subject and object are inextricably linked, there is a progressive *decentralisation of the subject*. This leads to a two fold activity: of externalization leading to physical objectivity and of internalization tending to logico-mathematical coherence. Physical knowledge remains impossible without the logico-mathematical framework, and it is impossible to conceive of the latter without it being applicable to 'any' object whatever.

Logical Operations and Language Development

It is significant that such reversible relationships as described in the Piagetian setting begin to be formed almost parallel to the linguistic development. The fact that language decontextualizes also appears to aid in the ability to make reversible relationships of the kind discussed above. Thus this particular ability seems at its best during adolescence where decontextualization is at its peak, in so far as the adolescent is now able to operate on the abstract level of theoretical assumptions.

Linguistic development, then, as we have seen also shows a parallel progress as in for instance the use of the word *because*. Upto the concrete operations stage, the child uses *because* to express a relation; he cannot explain the various possibilities of the relations. This is due to a lack of direction. The decline of ego-centrism and the growth of logical justification are part of the same process. In the sensori-motor or the ego-centric stage, there is lack of direction in thinking, owing to the fact that there is nothing here to make thought conscious of itself. Significantly such direction develops only late in the socialization of thought. Conceivably, then, language plays a crucial role in this socialization that is essentially *directive*, although Piaget himself makes no such assertions.

Implications for Schooling and Pedagogical Instruction

This exploration of the stagewise development of the child becomes necessary for the educational relevance it has in the context of schooling. There is a striking correspondence between the formal features of the adolescent responses and that which schooling produces.

The adolescent, as opposed to the child is committed to possibilities. Here is a person who can reflect. Yet the capacity for abstraction is at odds with the immediate society to which he must adapt. Formal thinking is both thinking about thought and a reversal of relations between the real and the possible. These two characteristics enable the adolescent to both live in society and beyond it. In this duality, the adolescent not only tries to adapt his ego to the environment but just as emphatically, tries to adjust the environment to his ego. This ego-centrism comes out, as Piaget, says in a sort of Messianic form such that he feels himself a reformer. The result is a relative failure to distinguish between his own point of view as an individual and the point of view of the group he hopes to reform. This is a significant point in our analysis of Progressivism as it will be seen later.

Bruner

Speaking more specifically about the function of language in cognitive development, Bruner, the educational psychologist argues that the use of language in ordinary discourse without exploitation of its inherent structure of meaning and organization, seems to have very little effect on the thought of its users beyond what might be called a 'species minimum'. Beyond this it is not so much the possession of language that matters but rather the elaboration of its use. Given the concrete, intuitive use of language, limited to matters of fact one cannot proceed beyond the Piagetian concrete operation stage. That is language will relate only to the local rather than universal, logical principles of relationships.

The Analytic Competence: Decontextualing Function of Language

According to Bruner (1975), it is only when one uses language beyond this level that it alters or indeed transforms the nature of thought processes in a significant manner. The most distinct feature of such language use is its movement toward context-free elaboration. The most dramatic step in this direction was the development of systems that rendered the spoken form into the graphic form. Again, the effective use of these systems works back a transformation of thought. For Bruner, there is beyond the linguistic and the socially reinforced communicative competence a third sphere in which language provides a new basis for the human invention of new models of thought. This, he terms as the *analytic competence.* Its principle feature as with Piaget's formal operations is that it involves the prolonged operation of thought processes exclusively on linguistic representations, on propositional structures, accompanied by strategies of thought and problem solving appropriate not to direct experience with objects and events but with *ensembles of propositions.* Most often than not, this competence generates symbol systems like mathematics or more powerfully elaborated forms of natural language like poetry.

The learning of a language of communication is a qualitatively different activity, says Bruner (1975), from learning to use language internally as a technique of representation. The important thing about language as an instrument of thought says Bruner, is not simply a translation of action into a new coin of words. Rather, "the new medium allows one to transform what one has to put into it into a new and powerful form that is not possible by other means". (Bruner: 1975) The production rules of language, its combinatorial richness, is potentially available as a means for going beyond experiences. In this sense it is a powerful tool for innovation.

Bruner (1975) refers to Vygotsky's "inner speech" as an example of speech that becomes embodied in thought. Inner speech, according to Vygotsky' is the opposite of Outer speech; outer speech being that which develops in interactions with others, " a turning of thoughts into words, its materialization and objectification", (Vygotsky: 1986) With inner speech, there is a reversal, speech turns into thought.

Consequently the structure must differ. Inner speech, according to Vygotsky (1986) is characterized by a prediction that totally omits the subject. The situation is similar to one where the perfect understanding between two people results in the omission of the subject. The subject is too familiar to be mentioned. Predication, then, is a technique of abbreviation. It is an abstract logical connection that does away with the concrete.

Such Predications, similar to the possibilities of Piaget's formal operations are characterized by strong inter connections, in contrast to the looseness of spontaneous speech. These possibilities are the lacks in primitive cultures due to which the Bernsteinian universal code fails to take root. This sense of possibility that nurtures the formal operations, either doesn't exist or is at best, degenerated in the primitive cultures.

Implications for Curricula

Concerned as he is with the pedagogical implications of such complex mechanisms, Bruner (1971) is convinced that the chief effect of schooling is to cultivate the language outside the context of action. Schooling, as he explores its functioning, seems to have a profound effect on a large number of mental processes, significantly with respect to the language learning faculty.

Attracted by the powers of analytic competence, Bruner lays down the guidelines for the curriculum that encourages and enhances this competence. Curricula should, according to Bruner (1969) include subjects introduced in a manner that is conducive to an inquiring mind. Such a mental makeup will not only enable a child simply to solve problems but also help to formulate them. Simply providing information in the behaviourist stance will only render the student passive. What is needed is active student participation through subject matter that is rendered accessible, manageable and at the same time interest-sustaining. Hypothesis making and testing should have an important place in Curricula.

The intuitive potential inherent in the student, says Bruner, should be exploited to the maximum by knowledge that he can have access to. A basic rule is to present issues in their most generalised form so that its relevance is not lost even beyond the present circumstances. In short, Curricula need to be structured in a manner that skill transfer becomes easy and learning retains relevance as well as economy.

Schooling which makes for such curricula progressively decontextualizes learning. It moulds the student and processes his mental framework in such a way as to enable him to operate on a conceptual level. This it does through its use of the symbolic system of language. While oral language retains its immediacy, by resorting to the written medium, the school progressively abstracts experience. Language in other words is used more in the mode of, "analytic competence" rather than merely communicative. Lacking this sophistication of schooling, language remains a concrete, world related, context-tied instrument for the unschooled child. It becomes a *restricted code* in Bernstein's words.

From within the realm of the *possible* as against the real on the other hand, there is virtually no limit for the ideals that the schooled adolescent can construct. This idealistic vision of the school pupil allows for an interpretation that is beyond the capabilities of the unschooled. This objective interpretation of the school Messiah allows him unwieldy control over his environment and results in an 'individualization' that becomes the brandmark of advanced technological civilization. From within this subjective world, the reformer Messiah makes history as he thrusts himself onto the world, and makes sense of it. On the other hand, the unschooled primitive, who often makes no distinction between the thing and its name, much like the child in Piaget's Sensori Operation stage, retains identity as a member of a tribe, context tied and powerless except within the limits set by the group.

Transmissions of such differentiated value systems, says Bruner, have their impact on future generations as well. Typically then, the middle class women who are themselves products of schooling encourage their children to question, to probe and patiently await the answer, while the working-class mothers, alienated from this mainstream resort to devices that yield to immediate satisfaction, discourage questioning and typically hand down what they themselves received. Yet, Bruner, hastily points out, there is in the primitive or in the economically backward no 'cultural deprivation'. Such lacks as is found in them could be thwarted effectively by what he terms 'community action', a moral gesture typical of the reformer that he has in mind.

Dewey: Liberal Humanism

Like Bruner, Dewey's (1916) democratic ideals appeal for an educational curriculum that is accessible to the child. According to Dewey, "the necessity of teaching gives an immense stimulus to reducing experience to that order and form which will render it most communicable and hence most usable."(1916) Education is of utmost necessity for Dewey if the young are to participate in the complexity of social life. But formal education may become too remote from the everyday experience of life. As societies become more advanced the need for formal teaching increases. In primitive societies, knowledge in its simple forms was close to the everyday life experience, therefore, the `idea' of a separate institution of schooling would have been preposterous. The danger then, as Dewey visualises, is the possibility of a growing split between the experience gained in more direct associations and that which is acquired in school.

The three important functions that Dewey (1916) holds important for the school are: (1) It provides a simplified environment to which the young can respond favourably. Through these simple forms it progressively leads the young to gain insights into the complex structures of societies. (2) The school is selective in so far as it filters out the undesirable features of the existing environment. It establishes a purified medium of action by such selection procedures, and reinforces the power of the best to make for a better future society. (3) It creates a wider and better balanced environment than would be possible if the young were left to learn by themselves. The school therefore, has the 'civilized' function of refining those crude impulses, one is born with.

Education basically consists in controlling and directing the crude animal impulses inherent in the human. A civilized social life calls for a harmonious relationship which would not be possible, if their impulses are allowed to freely act without some kind of an intrinsic control. Education provides this intrinsic control by giving insights into the commonality of interests that hold the society together.

In this attempt at directing the young through education, society determines its own future growth. Growth presumes immaturity, which has within it the potential for growth in its positive implications. Immaturity implies two basic tenets that of dependency and plasticity. The dependence, from the social stand point is infact a powerful device that involves interdependence and not a sign of helplessness. The ego-centricism of the child that is displayed is a social response employed on its own behalf. If the ends appear selfish, it is only because the adults have already mastered the ends and therefore can respond indifferently. Plasticity is the power to learn from experience. It includes the formation of habits:

both in this passive sense of acquiring routine activities as well as in the more dynamic sense of adaptability to new conditions of life. This adaptability partakes of an active involvement of thought, invention and initiative in applying virtual potential possibilities to new aims. Education in its attempt to direct the young exploits its potentials for growing towards a better social life.

The Child and the Curriculum

Dewey (1975) explores two schools of thought (1) that which emphasizes the psychological aspect of the child and appeals for education that is more organic and child centered (2) that, which emphasizes the refashioning of the child's crude impulses into perfect structures of logical reasoning. For Dewey, there is essentially no contradiction between the two modes of thought. He insists that these two ways of thinking really represent two points in the progressive educational process. To insist on the difference is to insist on the contradiction between the child and the mature adult. There is indeed a continual process of growth involved between the two phases. For Dewey, then, there is no opposition between the child and the educational curricula. Dewey insists that in the process of educating the child, experience needs to be simplified, psychologized as he terms it, before the child can assimilate it. This is the initial necessity of drawing him into the process of schooling. Nevertheless, as he advances, education should mould him into a logical reasoning human mind. Without such efforts, the child will remain self centered and irresponsible. Therefore, over indulgence in the child by catering to his organic needs will only lead to disaster. It requires the rigorous disciplines of logical subjects to mould the young.

The logical emphasis of the curriculum is therefore not set over the psychological. It is itself a point in the development process. As in the Pigetian setup, there is a gradual movement from the concrete to the formal operation stages. In Curriculum terms such a progress requires that the subject matter be made more organic, translated into the immediate relevance for the child. Such psycholozing takes place in the hands of the teacher. Failure to render it more organic results in the (1) lack of connection to the child's immediate experience (2) lack of motivation (3) the logic is lost on the child and becomes stuff for rote learning.

It is only when the curriculum is made accessible to the child by emphasis on the basic principles, as Bruner suggests, that the child is able to assimilate it into its mental structures. Only then can he/she progressively establish within his/her mental make up those ensemble of propositions that are the brandmark of analytic competence and hence of the rational mind.

A similar quest for the rational mind leads Hirst (1975) to the development of those modes of thought to which all efforts should be geared. These modes of thought are fundamental to the making of a rational mind. A specialization that restricts its boundaries and refuses the development of those fundamental modes is actually doing a disservice to the student. Pedagogical objectives, therefore need to be framed in a manner that shows the inter relationships between various modes of thought. It is, finally, these modes in their generalised form that help in ensuring a rationality that marks the cognitive growth of the child.

A Summing Up

Basically, then, as we have seen from the above discussion, the humanistic approach to education had important pedagogical implications. The most significant feature is the emphasis on the progressive development of the rational mind. Through the elaborate and symbolic system of language, schooling encourages mental processes that correspond to the cognitive development.

Language from the psychological perspective, as also from the educational point of view, aids in the development of thought and leads to a conceptual level of experience that has little to do with the immediate reality. Schooling on the other hand provides the necessary de-contextualisation through its promotion of language and makes for an individualization that holds sway over the outside world, subjective and objective alike, in its true humanist zeal for reform.

The Process Paradigm

In their pursuit of the 'rational mind' the humanists, it seems have gone beyond their subjective musings to establish a virtually unquestionable hegemonic domination of the human, more than compensating for the behaviourist reductionism.

Of crucial importance then, for the Progressive pursuit of the rational mind, are the pedagogical processes by which the school succeeds in achieving this end. In this context, the process of teaching, more so, the process of learning becomes very crucial. If the Behaviourist conviction of the teacher-model was modest, that of the Progressivist to make learning processes themselves potential resources for remodelling the learner is, to say the least, an ambitious project.

Interactive Setup

Such a *process* which involves both teachers and learners as co-producers in a classroom is basically an interactive setup, where the procedures of language learning or the very act of learning through such simple nuances as asking for clarification, turn taking, refusing to answer are significant indications of the cognitive development. It seems as if the intricate cerebral operations are being made explicit through such external cues. The significance stems from the fact that such processes that occur in the classroom involve a negotiation of meaning, the implications of which are partly contributed by the teacher, the class as a whole and by the learners' own potential resources. (Allwright, 1984). Very importantly, it involves the concept of learner management of learning (Allwright 1980) and throws the complete focus on the learner, almost as if he is being x-rayed. The Liberal humanist or the progressivist humanist of course, is careful to do so only within the precincts of the classroom, lest he is accused of a similar crime, committed by the Behaviourist, of projecting as natural, a habit cultivated by rigorous exercise.

The Communicative Framework

To trigger off these processes a communicative set-up is a must. Without communicative competence it is difficult to establish or even capture the cognitive signs of growth. If language development itself is taken to be evidence of cognitive growth, which implication is indeed very strong as Bruner suggests, (1975) then, communication indeed, is the most crucial part of the experiment. Ardent enthusiasts of the Process Curricula have identified this communication as basically oral, although it could also take the written form (as in task-based syllabuses) in so far it operates within the classroom boundaries.

The Classroom

From within the Process curriculum framework, Breen (1985) speaks of the classroom as an environment in itself, in which learners actively participate in processes of inquiry, discussion and reflection, rather than in confirmation to pre-determined objectives. Such processes render the behavioural outcomes of students unpredictable. There is, in these Process oriented syllabuses, an integration of context and experience. It is concerned as much with the learning experience of learners as with the subject matter content of these experiences.

The How vs What

In fact the content of any experience is bound up with the process of experience itself. To 'Know' content is to explore a methodology where content cannot reasonably be seen to exist independently of its interpretation. It is thus a syllabus of 'How' rather than 'What' and orients itself to those who interpret it; to the learner who along with his peers and teachers determines his own objectives and routes. This vested interest in personal objectives secures the relevance of the syllabus for the learner. From this perspective, the syllabus becomes a dynamic and negotiated concept rather than one which is static and imposed.

Problem Solving Approach

Such an interactive syllabus suggests a model which is social and problem solving in its orientation rather than one which transmits pre-selected knowledge. Hypothesis testing and hypothesis making, Bruner observes (1971), should be an essential factor of curriculum. The model, thus, becomes one in which participants, both teachers and learners are encouraged to ask questions about syllabus, context, methodology and their evaluation.

A model that encourages these aspects is appropriately realised through problem-posing tasks. The focus on problem solving with its implications for social negotiation among participants towards unpredictable outcomes will at best make for a retrospective record, not as a prospective plan. This is not to suggest, says Candlin (1985), that sequencing is unimportant, but as Allwright (1980) advocates, only that we should take them out of teacher's control. The Process approach lays emphasis on the uniqueness of each teaching/learning context. The progressivists concern for learners becoming responsible for their own teaching is paralleled by a similar concern for the teachers becoming responsible for improving their own Curriculum in the classroom.

The Foreign Language Curriculum: The Second Language Acquisition Research

Process approaches to the foreign language curriculum concentrate on creating the right environment for individual interlanguage development. The stress is less on syllabus definition and more on methodological principles of procedure designed to set the language learning process in motion. Concern for individual differences among learners is prominent. Attempts to develop strategies to respond to these differences are tirelessly worked out to promote the learners' sense of involvement.

The psycholinguistic hypothesis that underlines the Process approaches suggests that language acquisition is a subconscious process leading to the build up of an internal system. It has a developmental sequence, largely irrespective of the mother tongue, in which learners process or regress at different rates. Inter language, says Corder (Clarke 1971), is a continuum of more or less smooth change, and we can locate learners, like infants among the continuum.

Having already acquired an L1 it would seem as if the adolescent or adult learner has an apriori innate formal mechanism, that makes it more easy for him to understand language rules, unlike the child who is in still in Piaget's words the concrete operation stage. Because of the adult's ability to generalize and abstract, rule based instructions would be more understandable for him. The basic contradiction in this claim stems from the fact that language acquisition being a naturally sub-conscious process, explicit learning by rules cannot result in language learning. This is Krashen's contention. (1981) But where adult second language learners are concerned, Krashen does agree that explicit rules can help in language learning.

From this perspective errors are seen as points in the developmental sequence of language learning, and not as threats to be wiped out. However, the question as to whether or not to encourage formal learning of a language is an issue on which the Progressivists are divided. Discourse studies and information processing theories have however moved beyond the *formal* issue to highlight more crucial features as the *context, knowledge of the world* etc., much in the sense of Bruners' fundamental themes that become relevant beyond the present concerns. Processing which requires restructuring of existing schema may call for a rigorous bottom-up processing up as Clarke (1971) puts it, while more familiar tasks may require an alternate application of existing schemas.

Learners Strategies in Foreign Language Communication

In our attempts to communicate with others there is, in other words, a negotiation between the mental schema and the language we possess. When the language resource proves deficit other communicative strategies are called to compensate this lack. Learning to communicate effectively includes above all, that we confirm to certain maxims, some of which Grice elaborates as

- to say only which is necessary
- to say what we believe
- to be relevant
- to be clear and brief.

These maxims are more than relevant in the context of a foreign language learning; contexts where efforts to communicate are seen as including principles that promote acquisition as also the capacity to create and process discourse and negotiate meanings. Thus, as Breen, Candlin and Waters, observe, "rather than encourage learners to learn a language in order to communicate we may encourage learners to communicate in order to develop their learning." (Breen, Candlin: 1980) That the learner comes with certain communicative abilities must be recognised from the start. It is these abilities say Breen and Candlin (1980), which can be exploited to facilitate language learning. The learners ongoing process competence, as they put it, must be activated. If language is presented as if it were something static and not a developmental process, then, we most certainly postpone the development of the learners ability to communicate in the new language. (Candlin: 1985)

The Process paradigm accommodates not simply learners variability in terms of initial resources but also in terms of expectation. In fact, it is this variation that is its potential enrichment. Within the classroom arena, co-operative negotiations make for a joint interpretation and sharing of meaning. This kind of involvement exploits the productive relationship between using the language and learning the language. The classroom is no longer an apology for the authentic environment. In itself, it constitutes an authentic socio-cultural construct and refuses to be seen merely as a substitute for the native speakers' environment.

Linear Progression Broken

The process of learning and decision making (which is within the Process paradigm the learners own responsibility) does not proceed in a linear direction. In other words, there is no systematic stage-wise development that we are familiar with in the Piagetian cosmos. Dealing as we are with adults' who are already proficient speakers of their native language, such a precision can hardly be expected. The SLA research theories have now hinted at a natural sequence of development similar to native-language acquisition, though a fuller exploration is still awaited. There, appears to be a constant back and forth movement as the learner struggles to communicate in a new language. According to Dickinson (1987) choices are made along a forked path. In such a flexible setting, common objectives cannot exist. While this may appear chaotic initially, it reduces anxiety and the unhealthy competition and paves the way for individualisation within the classroom construct.

Towards the Autonomous Individual

Learner autonomy is virtually the mode of operation within the Process framework. Yet, this does not preclude the teacher from giving guidance when it is sought. In pursuing the 'processes' that ultimately lead to language learning, the Process proponent breaks down authority structures so predominant in the traditional curricula. Traditional syllabuses, says Candlin (1985) were prescriptions for action by teachers and learners. They have traditionally the mark of authority. The teacher in the Process framework, is more like Rogers', facilitator acting more as a moral support rather than the model of perfected language. In fact, he is as much of a learner himself as a teacher. The learner is free to ask for guidance in so far it helps him to perceive and pursue what Allwright (1982) terms as 'needs, wants and lacks'. The paradox, say Breen and Candlin (1985) lies in the fact that genuine independence arises only to the extent that it is interdependently granted. Within the Process syllabus, then, the negotiation role is, both public and private in so far as it happens within the learner and within the context of the classroom group. It therefore takes on the nature of an authentic communicative situation which is by nature intrapersonal and interpersonal in so far as it occurs both within the social setting and within one self. This '*Pedagogy*' has undoubtedly exploited and captured the individual in all his nuances and endowed him with powers unimaginable. So much so that it is difficult to predict the outcomes of this 'glorified' mind of the individual. In the public set up of the school, he is an enlightened learner. And within the privacy of his intellectual developments, he seems to wield uncontrollable power that threatens to swallow the less powerful section of humanity; the less intellectual. At the same time these 'processes' expose individual weakness and make more easy for the more intelligent to threaten the less so. Democratic tendencies in such settings serve only to reaffirm the success of the more intelligent (as this is defined by the educational institution) on the one hand, while it individualises the failures of the intellectually weak. In fact, the complexity of the relationships that the Process achieves make it impossible for the intelligent learner to fix responsibility. The maze of processes leads him into evermore darker regions, from where there seems to be no return. In the wake of such an event, human fate would be the worse for us; for, unlike the behaviorist who used rats and rabbits for his experiments, our reformer humanist uses the less intelligent human being for the same purpose.

Conclusion

The pedagogy described in this Chapter has undoubtedly explored the learners individual powers to the extreme. Yet the Piagetian studies are limited to children of his own family. Similarly, Bruners' Curriculum proposals do not take the learners social status into consideration. Again, Dewey's rejection of the barriers between child and

Curriculum throws no light on the kind of learner he has in mind.

In failing to locate the learner in his social set up, the Progressivists make for an *idealised Curriculum* meant for an *ideal learner*. Distance systems which pledge to cater to the disadvantaged learner have to necessarily take the 'social' factors into account. It is only as the Distance systems grapple with these social structures in which the learner finds himself entangled, that significant implications for the curriculum can emerge. Specifically with regard to language curriculum Distance systems may have to take special note of the learners status in society, the purposes for which he needs the language, and the status accorded to this language specifically within a particular context and more generally to the nation to which he belongs. The interactive environment that the Distance acknowledges then, is not the stimulus described by the behaviourists or the supportive environment of the Piagetian setup but the more complex power structures that society creates.

Multiple as they are, these social structures call for different kinds of Curricula. On the sociological side, learner diversity, will in itself demand variations in the Curriculum. Therefore, Distance systems having to deal with this complex network of societies and individuals within them cannot afford to opt for the easy solution of an *ideal Curriculum* for the *ideal learner*.

2

From Pedagogy to Androgogy

This Chapter moves from the pedagogical to the androgogical situation to explore similar issues relating to the learner, the autonomy that the learner enjoys and the curriculum that makes allowance for these aspects in its official format. The Chapter begins in defence of Pedagogy, where it is stated that since the learner is only a child, it may be essential to hold on to certain assumptions or idealized versions of the learner and the learning situations. If only for the purposes of setting directions, such ideals serve to set definite goals towards which one can strive.

The Chapter explores and describes adult education as characteristically different from pedagogy. The adult, it is suggested is not a child, and therefore the assumption that the learner is cognitively immature is an unacceptable notion. Therefore, it is argued, that there is no contradiction between the learner and the teacher, at least, in terms of learning experiences. Learning becomes important for the adult only because he feels the need to boost his career or needs or to update his knowledge. From here, the chapter tends to identify the adult learner. There is, then, a discussion of the adult characteristics, in terms of who exactly the learner is, the differences between the learner and the teacher as also the fact that he has a rich experience on which to draw on. These features have a direct relevance to the Distance Mode of education. Other aspects related to the cognitive development in the adult, and the concept of autonomy are also discussed.

Traditional educational systems, it is stated, emphasized the adult characteristics, thus giving it the psychological bias earlier noticed, in pedagogy. Autonomy, the traditional educationists seem to assert, is something that comes naturally to the adult. Welcome as this conclusion is for the Distance Mode, it necessarily has to place the adult in a given socio-economic context. Adulthood becomes problematic as it depends on what exactly is considered adulthood in different social contexts. Similarly, although .individualisation is and should be the basic mode of operation, given the Distance Mode, the social context of large populations and the limited resources in which the distance systems function, ironically make way for standardization. Caught in this dilemma, Distance Education has yet to come to terms with a Curriculum that is acceptable both to the individual and the society at large.

Similar implications are worked out for the language Curriculum. The adult psyche, it is asserted, should be given due consideration. It is within this context that instruction becomes important. Curriculum implications that emerge in the traditional system of education are equally valid to the distance mode, in so far as the learner in both systems is an adult. However the definite move of distance education to place the adult in a given social context, that partakes of his occupation, his contribution to the society and above all his aspirations to reach higher levels in the social hierarchy ask for a redefinition of androgogy.

In Defence of Pedagogy

To a large extent, it is only understandable that education especially, in a pedagogical situation should be more conservative. In so far as the school is a relatively autonomous institution, it needs to preserve what Bernstein (1975) calls the *expressive order* that gives it an ethic of its own to carry out the noble function of refining crude impulses for egalitarian purposes. That inequalities exist, despite the democratic tendencies that the school promotes, could be accounted for by the fact that such inequalities remain invisible. Since the immediate impact of such inequalities does not become obvious until much later in life, they tend to remain *invisible*.

It is also true that at this stage of life where economic differences have little relevance, such inequalities take the shape of more culture bound attributes such as dress habits, style of speaking and so on. While these factors have a strong influence, they are not penalized for what they are, but remain under covert reasons as *non-achievement*. This makes more meaningful the fact that the economically deprived but culturally less so are more at an advantage than those who are substandard in both the economic and the cultural aspects.

Freire's Adult Education: Collaboration in Learning

When it comes to adult education, the first aspect that seems to have caught attention is the fact that the educational system catering to the adults must have the necessary means to deal with a mature and responsible mind. The educational institution must respect the mature characteristics of the adult, if it has to succeed in its mission. Just as it was important to take cognizance of the psychological development of the child, so it is important to cater to the mature psyche of the adults.

The experiential maturity of the adult defies any attempt to treat him as if he were a child. In so far as this experiential reality of the mature adult is taken account of, he is not the *empty vessel* receiving information from the teacher, who is the epitome of knowledge and authority. Freire visualizes the educational system as a parallel to the colonial system. In so far as education is posited as an ethical institution, it becomes an authoritative structure where the teacher presumptuously posits himself as a knower, while the student is the ignorant soul. Such a presumption, says Freire, is a violation of humanity.

The Banking Concept

In the concept of education, *knowledge is a gift* bestowed by the teacher on the student who knows nothing. Knowledge as a process of inquiry is totally negated in this perspective, which is characteristic of the ideology of oppression. The teacher colonial, through this attitude, destroys and dehumanizes the learner and holds. him in a subject/object relationship. According to Freire, (1983) men mediate with reality and transform it in the process of making history. Men are historical beings who live in time and make sense of a past, present and future as opposed to animals which are ahistorical. Yet the teacher colonial having denied the student historicity and reduced his experiences to nothing, feels free to impose his interpretation on the student. In the non-acknowledgement of this critical consciousness in the student, the meaning given by the teacher is the *truth*.

True education, says Freire (1983) must dissolve this contradiction of the teacher and the student, so that both are simultaneously the teacher and the student. A true relationship calls for a horizontal basis, not a top-down hierarchy. The teacher has to establish a dialogical relationship with the students and not of *the haves and the havenots*. A truly human relationship can emerge only through communication; through recognition of people as conscious beings and not as objects.

Problem-Posing Education

The truly committed, says Freire, must reject the banking concept of education and replace it with the problem posing education. Liberal education should consist in *acts of cognition* not a transfer of information. Problem-solving education which responds to this cognition and establishes meaning in the human effort to relate, asks for the dissolution of the teacher-student contradiction. Such a dialogical relation makes for a new term, the teacher-student or the student-teacher. The teacher is no longer the one who teaches but someone who also learns in the process of relating to the student. The students teach while being taught. Education in Freire's terms, then, is a continuity, a never-ending process, a historical process. This is particularly relevant to the adult-learner.

Lifelong Education

In the adult learner is an entity which forces us to rethink and reorganize our views of education and the processes by with it is propagated. The banking system has had deep-seated roots, so that adult education tends to be treated in a manner similar to that of child education. This has been a basic hindrance to the programme of adult education. Granted that education is a *continuous process* the 20th century has added further dimensions by invalidating knowledge acquired in the past and replacing it with concepts which are relevant in the present. Adult learning, then, has found it justification in attempting to update its knowledge and be in the Main Stream of the historical process.

The Adult Learner/Who is He?

Who is the adult learner? Many have attempted to describe him. Adult learning mainly refers to "individually planned learning in any area of interest, undertaken for practical purposes or for pleasure or curiosity". (Daniel John ed. 1982). The definition adds that the learner will more than in the past be *female*. Why do adults learn?

Statistics has shown that while many of them learn for the sake of learning, for the majority of them, the purpose is utilitarian. There is further evidence to show that the prevalence of learning is highest among the professionals, the white-collared, skilled workers rather than the blue-collared unskilled workers. Education seems to have become an indivisible part of ideological literature that serves only a certain section of the society. The deschooling of education has yet a long way to go before it reaches the community of peasants whom Freire speaks of. To the extent that it has made place for the adults, who have upto this point been eliminated from the educational mainstream, this is, however an optimistic sign.

Androgogy: Adult Characteristics

Shouldn't the educational system which is basically a pedagogical system then re-align itself to accommodate the adult learner? The process of education in the form of the banking system has continued to live despite its irrelevance in this context. Unlike the child who is in a sense dependent on the teacher, and is distanced from him, by way of age and experience, the adult learner is on par with the teacher on both these grounds. This is precisely why it is necessary for us to reorient our thinking and take into consideration some basic assumptions regarding the adult. It is for example, as Knowles (1983) puts it, necessary for us to realize that here is a person:

(1) who has developed a self-concept, a mature person fully conscious of his responsibilities, towards his family, to his institution and therefore, to a large extent self-directing.

(2) who expects to be acknowledged and respected as an equal and who feels depressed, when his experiences are not recognised.

(3) whose learning strategies are basically different from those of a child, in the sense that he is more conscious

of the immediate relevance of the problems to his own situation.

In a teaching situation these factors have to be taken into consideration. At the same time, allowance has to be made for the fact that as soon as the adult finds himself in a classroom situation he expects to be taught like a child. Therefore, working with the adults, means attempting to resolve these contradictions which are partly inherent in the system and partly in the learner himself.

The deficiencies or the blocks that the adult learner sets up for himself in the form of set habits as Knowles says, can, to a large extent be removed by building up a relationship of trust, of giving him the feeling that we are working with him and not for him. In Freire's terms, at no moment should the teacher attempt to lecture to him. The moment he does so, even if inadvertently, he negates the very purpose of the revolution. Androgogy shares some of its features with Allen Tough's (Griffin 1983) research into adult learning. Tough is concerned with the vast area of self-directed learning that goes on quite outside the formal organisation of adult education.

Rogers: The Encounter-Group

Yet another strategy in keeping with the adult psychology is Rogers' (1983) Encounter-Group. In this group members interact with one another and in the process of interaction get over past experience and accommodate new ones. He calls for the whole person learning which makes allowances for both cognitive and affective factors. Rogers also allows for physical responses and those other features which lead to learning in stress free environment.

Paterson's Knowledge Modes for the Adults

Paterson, (Griffin: 1983) who takes a philosophical view of knowledge like Hirst and Peters, suggests that education is a process of induction into the public forms and modes of knowledge, the aim of which is a worthwhile state of mind. For Paterson, then, adult Curriculum, in order to count as education must be a kind of selection from among the many forms of knowledge. Most exponents of the adult Curriculum characteristically insist on the basic psychological differences between the child and the adults as the distinguishing feature of adult education. They are, however, deviant on the exact nature of these differences. For Paterson, this takes the form of certain trends of cognitive development, yet he also speaks of the distinctiveness of adult education in terms of maturity. There seems to be a confusion between forms of knowledge valuable in themselves and those that are distinctly meant for the adults.

Professional Service & Adult Learning

Another important approach that concentrates on the adult characteristics has arisen out of the process of professionalisation itself. This essentially views adult education as a structure of provision for meeting adult learning needs. It calls for a more professional strategy. There is a kind of overlap between the categories of professional service and adult learning. Graham Mec (cited in Griffin, 1983) who resorts to this view, is more concerned with adult education as an object of professional design that has more to do with organisational and management theory. He places emphasis on aspects of openness, accessibility and relevance of the provisional system to adult learners.

Cognitive Development of Adults: Allman

Reflection on adult education has also brought into focus the whole question of cognitive development in the adults. In his last writings, Allman says, (1983) Piaget predicts certain changes that would take place in the formal operations stage due to the influence of the socio-economic factors. This would result in the adaptation of the thinking processes. Allman considers Riegel's Theory (1973) of dialectical operations to be the most central of all the recent theories. The theory has its roots in the contextual paradigm, according to which, the thinking processes' of adults are directly influenced by inter-action with the socio-economic and historical contexts. This has echoes of the Friereian philosophy.

Since the historical process is always a continuing one, it is impossible to predict the most adaptive competencies. In other words, human cognition cannot be defined or fixed at any point of time. Man's subjectivity and historicity prevents him from such fixation. In Reigel's theory, Allman observes, contradiction is the most essential feature. Here again, we sense the Freirian undertones which posit man as a historical being relating to his environment in a dialectical manner.

For Reigal, Allman observes, the most important feature that causes the adult learner to progress, is his ability to ask questions or pose problems. He is, in other words, able to tolerate contradictions and allow problems to emerge. This however, Allman observes "does not mean that the dialectic thought never reaches a state of equilibrium but when it does it is a resting point, a temporary resolution, rather than an immutable structure". According to Reigal, adult thinking entails a reuniting of thought with reality, a reuniting of the abstract thought of the adolescent period with concrete reality.

This leads to the hypothesis that adult thought is qualitatively different from that of the adolescent. He is endowed with the critical ability, to look at his own thoughts, or to be *metatheoretical*, something that the adolescent cannot do. Further, although he has no memory for detail, he is capable of relating the general principles which according to Bruner (1969) is an important aspect of discovery learning.

Ego development, then, is not simply a biological outcome of a certain stage of cognitive development. It involves complex processes. In fact, we cannot speak of a stage theory in terms of the adult learner. He is the historical being in constant negotiation with the reality around him. From this perspective, then, the teacher-student relationship can be described more on a dialectical level, where the developmental superiority of the teacher is always in question.

The Question of Autonomy

Conceding these cognitive developments in the adult, should we then grant him autonomy as a student, where he can set his own pace of learning, can evaluate, and can make decisions regarding what he needs to learn. This brings into focus, the whole question of independent study in distance education. People who argue for autonomy justify it on the ground that, to limit the adult learner's freedom would be to encroach upon his strategy of learning and would be against the spirit of distance education. People who criticize it point to the heavy drop out rate which renders useless all attempts to promote distance education. Carl Rogers (1983) opts for a completely student-centered approach where the student has the freedom to learn whenever he wants and in whatever way he wants. He is more interested in the process of discovery-learning that Bruner describes, in which the adult is more successful than the adolescent, as he has a general feel for principles. Rogers shows little interest in the well-structured knowledge, which Ausubel (Cited in Baath: 1979) prefers. Such a process of discovery not only helps a person to learn, but also tells him about how to learn and how to solve new problems. The aim of education in the final analysis is self-realization. For Rogers, learning is experiential, self-initiated and self-evaluated. It's essential meaning is self-realization. Therefore learning is basically non-directive.

Distance Education: Role of Teacher

The teacher, for Rogers, is not an instructor but a facilitator who like Freire's co-ordinator is a decentralised figure. For Michael Moore (1983), the role of the teacher is simply to provide the environment where each individual learner is able to identify what he is ready to learn. This leads to what is called self-directed learning. Individualization and dialogue are crucial features in Moore's study. "A programme was said to be individualized to the extent to which a learner could control the pace at which he received information, while the dialogue described the extent to which the technological media made it possible for the learner to interact with the teacher"(1983). The media has played a very important role in this individualization process. Coldeway (Daniel ed. 1982) compared the Instructional Systems Design (IST) to Distance Education. The two are more or less based on similar assumptions of (1) The Individualized Instruction. (2) Self-pacing and so on. Modern computers offer a wide potential for such individualized instruction.

Androgogy/Pedagogy Compared

Learner autonomy, where the learner is able to determine the selection of objectives, resources, procedures and the evaluation design and measure his achievements, obviously assumes the behaviour of a mature adult. It also calls for some kind of emotional independence. Androgogy, then, as we have seen, seeks increasing amounts of self-direction. Pedagogy concentrates on content, while Andro-gogy focuses on tasks. In the Pedagogical model the teacher determines Curriculum teaching methods and evaluations whereas, the androgogical model stresses the importance of the teacher, as an agent in helping the learner participate in educational alternatives and make maximum use of all the elements available for teaching and learning. Knowles' concept of androgogy and his basic distinction between Pedagogy and Androgogy is largely misunderstood. The vast majority of distance education institutions have never attempted to engage in any type of interaction with learners that could be classified as Androgogical.

There is also, the inherent problem with the learners. Very few have had sufficient experience of Androgogy to adapt readily to a totally androgogical system. Almost everyone has grown up in a pedagogical system and require a total reorientation to overcome this internalized mechanism. Ideally, if autonomous behaviour is the quality of a mature adult, then, the very nature of good adult education is the restoration of learner autonomy.

Individualization vs. Standardization

Learning, then becomes an individual affair. Wedemeyer (1983) defends this individual enterprise as an expression of the individual will and individual competence which have to be recognized. If there are capitalistic overtones in his assertion, then, says Wedemeyer, they cannot be helped. To kill individual enterprise merely on the ground that they do not conform, is similar to the racial bias. While Freire (1983) talks of one kind of solidarity which involves all individuals in a dialectical kind of relationship, here is Wedemeyer upholding the prowess of the individual enterprise that the capitalist is familiar with.

If, says Wedemeyer, the individual has earned the right to be on the top, why not let him be there and give him credit for it? Why should he be usurped or enter into a relationship with the ordinary, where he remains discredited? "Curiously", says Wedemeyer, "there is some opposition to the concept of independent learning by social egalitarians, who seem to fear individual enterprise, even in learning". Learning, he says, is personal, idiosyncratic. What we need is a system of evaluation common for all learning systems and not the predominance of one over another.

Wedemeyer appeals for a non-biased approach to non-traditional type of learning. The fact that an individual has opted by his own endeavour to climb up should not go against him. Wedemeyer's view, has echoes of the Puritan work ethic. The view, however would not, be accepted by the leftists who argue that it is not the man of endeavour but a man with advantages who succeeds.

In fact this is exactly the contradiction inherent within the system of the distance education as a mode of instruction. While it claims to make allowance for individual variability, is it in fact catering to a kind of massification that Peters (1983) hints at? Otto Peters describes the distance education system as the most industrialized form of education; industrialized in the sense that it caters to the most scientific and rationalized way of educating people. According to Peters, the didactical structure of Distance Education can be best understood from industrialized principles, especially those of productivity, division of labour and mass production.

The mechanization of teaching methodology and the dependence of teacher effectiveness on prior planning and organisation posits a very objective and neutral role for the teacher. He characterizes the teacher/learner relationship thus:

(1) as being controlled by technological rules.
(2) maintained by emotion-free language.
(3) based on a limited possibility of analysing student needs and giving them directions.
(4) achieving its goal by efficiency.

Peters sees parallels between distance education and industrialization which make it the most suitable form of education for the modern times. Whether he is advocating it or is only describing a situation as relevant to our time, remains a matter for conjecture.

The totally dehumanizing texture of the system, its neglect of individuals as human subjects inevitably leads to visualize it as a kind of massification. Although Peters argues that the term *mass trend* is devoid of negative implications, in the new context of industrialization, one does not feel very convinced. If, then, finally we destroy the very thing we have been fighting to keep alive, namely, our subjective consciousness to be critical, isn't it a contradiction in terms? Will such a massification lead to a qualitatively better kind of education, a better individual or will it simply produce more and more goods for the capitalist; the goods from which the worker feels totally alienated?

Interpreted in this manner Pedagogy and Androgogy become synonymous. Seen as an industrial enterprise, the educational framework, builds up yet another dimension to the colonial system, where the adult learner is tamed or allows himself to be tamed and treated like the child in the pedagogical system. It forces the adult to conform to a standardization which kills all individual initiative. In so conforming to a set standard, the adult learner's experiential reality is totally negated. Industrialization or standardization of education leads to a uniformity which ignores individual variability. This conformity which is at a certain stage internalized by the adult, submerges him into an unquestioning impassive object.

Pedagogy, then, is essentially setting directions for the individual, without recognizing the fact that the individual has the experiential maturity to choose for himself. It is here that the adult learner's critical consciousness should urge him to question this situation. In continuation of the Piagetian ethic and the essentially liberal stance that these adult characteristics approaches take, the adolescent adult's critical consciousness should urge him to question this situation and enable him to see his situation as *problematic*. Only here can we foresee the true androgogical implications emerging.

Adult Education: A Matter of Technique

This focus on the adult characteristics has been of crucial importance to the programme of adult education. The psychological import of the adult experience is of prime significance. While the adult has a repertoire of experience, the child has comparatively few. Therefore, in approaching these two entities there ought to be significant methodological difference. In so far as the adult needs to be weaned away from fixed notions and remoulded to be open to new interpretation, the techniques employed essentially differ from those that come into play during the developmental stages of childhood. Thus in androgogy and other approaches which emphasize on this methodological difference, on the basis of adult characteristics, adult education is a means for self-realization, almost Nirvana like experience.

The Psychological Bias: Reaffirmation of the Pedagogical Stance

Although at first sight these approaches that insist on the *adult characteristics* appear different from the pedagogical situation, basically as we shall see, they call for a continuation of the Piagetian ethic. In other words, they partake of the Progressive stance in reinforcing this qualitative difference between the child and the adult. The adult is the Piagetian adolescent in the formal operations stage. Here is a person who can make abstract logical relationships without the concrete presence of objects. Here is the ideal theoretical reformer who is capable of visualizing experiences and creating an ideal. Yet, here again is the adult who is very much in touch with the real as much as he is with the abstract. It is in this interactionary set-up that the adult posits himself. It is precisely this set-up that makes it particularly congenial for learning activities, especially, second language learning.

Implications for Language Learning

Concerned as it is with adult education, distance education has to take particular note of the various nuances that lead to second language learning in the adult. The purely psychological focus predominant in the Progressive rhetoric is particularly significant, as we begin to explore the differences between adult language learning and child language acquisition. Conscious application of rules seems more accessible to the adult than to the child. Therefore formal instruction, which is totally rejected in the case of the child is given due allowance with regard to the adult. (Krashen: 1961).

The SLA Research

The emphasis in SLA research on individual differences and factors like motivation, inhibition and anxiety levels are clearly relevant in the case of the adult learner who has in a way already formed his patterns of response. Significantly, the lower the inhibition, the more successful he is in learning the language. So also, the lower the filter, the more possibility of learning. Inter-language studies further, have to do with the structuring and the restructuring processes that take place during the language learning activity of the adult.

Errors which emerge out of the interaction of a previously patterned language facility with the newly learnt one, are positive signs of language acquisition. These same errors were treated as mistakes in the behaviourist era which they then sought to wipe out through forming new habits. These observations are in a sense reinforced by Cummins (1986), research in the field of bilingualism. According to Cummins, proficiency in the native language is a necessity in order to acquire second language. The threshold competence that is acquired in the first language makes it possible to learn a second language without much difficulty. However, in cases where this level is not reached in the native language, competence in the second language will also suffer subsequently. This cognitive capacity is considered essential for the second language learner.

A similar rationale supports the procedural syllabus design. A task-based syllabus, says Prabhu, in which meaning or the message is of utmost importance, unconsciously contributes to building up a grammatical system. Therefore, the focus is not the formal aspects of language, but the meaning. Accordingly, Prabhu takes recourse to tasks based on activities of different kind which he variously terms, reasoning gap, opinion gap, information gap, information transfer, and so on. Of particular interest, he says, are the reasoning gap activities in which the information is proc ed in such depth that it activates the language learning faculty.

All these observations are relevant to the distance education mode, particularly, in relation to language learning. However, in as much as these approaches place so much emphasis on the psychological development, they are limiting. In so far as they do not take account of the socio-cultural factors, they say a half-truth. The other-half, as Durkheim says (1956) lies in the sociological analysis of a given situation in which the learner finds himself. It is from this angle that education, needs to be interpreted.

As we have seen, education for the Progressivist has remained of universal importance. So much so that it seems to have lost its social character. Almost rigorous in its utopian ideal, the liberal stance divorces education from its particularistic implications and elevates it to that of a universal phenomenon. In thus legitimizing it, it ignores those for whom it has less or no relevance.

Conclusions

This chapter investigated the androgogical situation, mainly to draw implications for the Distance Education, which is also concerned with the adult. However, the purely psychological bias of the traditional curricula make for an incomplete description of the learning process. A similar sense of incompleteness also informs the language Curriculum, which merely aims at a psychologically mature individual with little regard for his social status. Thus, although Distance Education Curriculum profits from psychological insights, it leaves more to be explored, especially in sociological aspects.

3

Early Sociological Research: The Correspondence Principle

Chapter two looked at Androgogy to highlight those aspects of adult education that are directly relevant to the distance mode. It has already been suggested that Androgogy and Distance System are similar in so far as they are concerned with the adult learner. Similarities are also perceived to the extent that both approaches have to make allowance for the psychological differences between the child and the adult. Yet such differences have merely limited themselves to the level of technique in adult education, while the distance mode has to go beyond this to explore the possibility of differences in content too.

The distance mode defines the adult learner as one who has a definite position in society and who is capable of affecting the productivity of that society through a particular kind of occupation. To the extent that these features have the potential to change his location in society and move him/her up in the social hierarchy, this adult is qualitatively different from the apolitical adult projected in androgogy. Locating this adult requires us to explore the sociological framework.

The chapter begins by analyzing the pedagogical stance which, it suggests, makes for an individualism, through emphasizing the psychological to the exclusion of all other dimensions. This individualism, an indication, and embodiment of power, it argues, enables the privileged to control the less so. In discussing androgogy, this chapter asserts that a similar psychological bias renders adult education a mere technical issue, what otherwise should be crucially a problematic. The two issues namely Pedagogy and Androgogy, it is stated, should be interpreted by access to the sociological perspective.

In introducing the sociological perspective, the chapter touches upon major trends in sociology, which include the Durkheimian position, and other developments that emerged as a reaction to positivism of Durkheim. In the section that follows, the chapter looks at the Correspondence principle, as one particular sociological perspective that strongly holds the school as responsible for sustaining inequalities existing in society. Although basically, the Correspondence principle refers to Pedagogy, one can stretch its implications to the androgogical situation. In so doing the distinctions between the mainstream curricula and the lower stream curricula, become obvious.

Repressive Pedagogy

The Progressive stance in both the pedagogical as well as the androgogical situation has been consistent in the sense, that it has tended to emphasize a strong psychological base for its argument. This psychological bias makes for an individualism that the more powerful exerts over the less so. The school then encourages one particular class of individuals over another. It protects the privileged class interests of one group, the more powerful over the less so.

Neo-Marxist critics like Apple, Bowles and Gintis and many others see the school as essentially a correspondent of society in preserving the inherent inequalities and biases prevalent in society at any given point of time.

From Pedagogy to Androgogy: Repressive Continuum

A similar Correspondence informs the programme of adult education. Catering to the psychological maturity of the adult as different from the child, androgogical implications retain significance as methodological principles. In so doing curricular categories of schooling are reproduced. This is despite the influence of writers such as Illich and Freire. The attempt to distance adult education from schooling through distinguishing adult characteristics has depoliticized the curriculum practices, as it fails to take account of these adult characteristics in relation to the definition, distribution and evaluation of knowledge, as they most visibly occur in any particular society as mainstream and lower stream education.

A similar preoccupation with needs as was noted earlier, reproduces the curriculum of schooling despite its potential to transform it. Adulthood is more problematic than the mere technique to which it gets reduced. Thus, Paterson's analysis makes for an awkward juxtaposition of conceptual thinking and an uncritical view of adulthood, while, Knowles's concept of the self and self-directed learning, seem at best abstractions. Adulthood, it is now acknowledged, is a social status. The concept of self direction, aspiration or needs depends very much on the individual's cultural and structural location in society.

Further as Griffin (1983) points out, despite the effort to differentiate pedagogy from androgogy, there seems to be no dynamic relationship between the two. Is pedagogy necessary to stimulate androgogy or do they simply coexist. As it stands, the theory seems to support the view that pedagogy stands for the powerlessness of the learner and androgogy for the learner's autonomy. But power and autonomy are social dimensions of a situation which require to be explored in the context of knowledge, culture and politics.

The Need for Sociological Research

To unravel these questions it becomes necessary for us to investigate research into the sociological perspective. Over the years, sociology has developed with distinct trends, some leaning towards positivist conclusions, while others concentrated on the interactionist perspective, including the phenomenological perspective. We shall now look at some of these basic trends to get an idea of how exactly such research developed.

Some Major Trends in the Sociology of Education/Knowledge

A dominant feature of the context of all contemporary research in the sociology of education is the controversy between scientific positivism and the reaction to it, notably from phenomenological and ethnomethodological approaches; the conflict between the normative and interpretative perspectives. Again there is the conflict between value-free and value-oriented sociology. Both these are central to sociological research as a whole.

The influence of the psychological interpretation of the pure science model on sociology is unquestionable. Only by demonstrating empirically, that there are laws governing human behaviour in societies could sociology claim for a legitimate existence. This pure science model of sociology represented by Durkheim (1956) with its reliable definitions, orders and control of materials and the detached behaviour of investigators has been largely responsible for the establishment of sociology as a subject of universal study.

Early Sociological Approaches: Durkheim (1956)

One of the starting points of the sociology of education was the functional analysis of education that the Durkheimian thought represented. The central function of education for Durkheim, like for Dewey, is socialization; a methodical preparation of the young for adult life. Yet, this social life is itself differentiated in so far as there is occupational diversity and education is correspondingly diversified as it prepares the young to fit these diverse patterns. Education is a social construct. To find an egalitarian education one has to go back to prehistoric societies which represent only a single logical point in the history of humanity.

Despite the educational differentiation based on occupational diversity, there is a common base that holds society together. It's object is to arouse in the child a number of physical intellectual and mental states that are demanded of him by both the political society as a whole and the special group for which he is specifically destined. This education being socially defined anyone who flouts it to the extreme will be surely penalised.

It is idle, says Durkheim, to think that we can rear children as we like. We are bound by social customs. Through education, transmission of social life is effected. While education can develop natural potentialities, it basically answers societal necessities. Therefore, it serves different needs in different societies. Yet in no way does it make man subservient, for men themselves willingly submit to this socialization. The legacy of human tradition is preserved says Durkheim, precisely because it is a social construct. There is thus no antagonism between the individual and society. Echoeing Dewey, Durkheim asserts that education makes for growth in a truly human manner. Education is essentially directive. Pedagogically this has relevance for the fact that it should be based on observable facts and that any hesitancy on the part of the educational authorities would be disastrous. A scientific mind is essential even in formulation of pedagogies.

Points for Pedagogy

Traditionally, all pedagogical statements have, Durkheim says, described what ought to be rather than what is. They are basically ideas, practical ones which have future orientation. Basically borrowing from psychological and sociological research, pedagogy needs to reflect them to meet current needs. It is only through reflection that one can prevent education from degenerating into habit. Such reflection calls for a historical perspective of education which alone can determine the educational ends.

Curriculum Implications

Though Durkheim discusses education as a whole rather than formal schooling, it would not be too difficult says Eggleston (1977) to build on his work to suggest a functional view of curriculum. Curriculum, in Durkheim's terms, would introduce pupil to experience, that anticipates their adult role; it makes for anticipatory socialization; it also makes for acceptance of differentiation where the curriculum legitimates the differences between students but also in the adult society. The curriculum here underpins the power structure of the society.

Limitations of the Durkheimian Position

Yet, as sociological analysis, the functional perspective is limiting. It rests on assumptions which are questionable. It assumes that the curriculum is a unified and coherent mechanism in a consensual world. The distinction observed between *official curriculum* and the *hidden curriculum* suggests that this is fallacious; there is conflict here as also within the official curriculum itself. In reality, there is no necessary consensus concerning aims, methodology or indeed any aspect of the curriculum within a school, let alone within a system.

Yet another point of criticism is the functional approaches tendency to take problems as *given* to define the behaviours and interaction norms, and goals. In the study of equality of opportunities, for example, it has taken *as given* the teacher's definition of opportunity and achievement instead of viewing them as problematic. According to Young (Eggleston: 1977) problems cease to be problematic when they are taken as given. It is, therefore, important to be aware of the perceptions that the participants bring to the curriculum–their social constructions of reality. Only then it will be possible to consider the realities of social behaviour associated with the curriculum. The constructions of reality of the student and of the teacher must have some area of congruence, if the curriculum needs to be operated. There are instances of dissonance, yet acceptance is easily learnt. But the fact that students give an acceptable performance does not necessarily modify their alternate constructions of reality.

The same problem may be seen at the macro level of society where crucial curriculum issues such as deprivation and educational opportunity are defined in terms of the powerful middle class. In so doing, according to Brandis and Henderson (1977), the statements regarding the working class appear as a deficit or deprivation, as compared to the standards achieved by the middle class itself. Such comparisons, tend to become evaluative in terms of better or worse, and puts the working child at a disadvantage by inevitably showing what the middle class can do and what the working class cannot do in relation to the middle class. This research which takes problems as given reinforces the social distinctions and reifies it as the ways things are.

Alternate Approaches

The consideration of alternative approaches to reality may be seen as a reaction to the Durkheimian positivism. Yet a total relativism cannot substitute the positivist attitude. The sociologist is basically concerned with the regularities and shared patterns of human behaviour. His enthusiasm to explore the individual's social construction of reality is to learn more about these regularities than before. The need is particularly crucial when one deals with the human behaviour that surrounds the school curriculum. For here, the official view of the curriculum, as was observed, is likely to be an incomplete one. The non-positivist approaches are valuable in so far as they help to achieve a fuller sociological analysis of the school curriculum.

The scientific conception of the every day world that had to be adopted in order to act in a scientific way was at variance with the subtle, shifting and often covert every day conceptions of the human world and the responses it evokes. The dissonance between methodology and subject matter became manifest. It was seen that even the attempt to act in a scientific way led to a necessary exclusion of some data and an ensuring over-weighting of other data. Research findings, says Eggleston (1974), must not only present findings but must also carry an interpretation, not only in the conclusions but in the very collection and analysis of the data. Eggleston quotes Kuhn as suggesting that the natural scientists themselves are limited by the paradigms of scientific knowledge which have an important influence on their choice of problems, research methodology and their analysis of results.

In an attempt to break through the barriers established as a result of the pure science/psychological research model, sociologists have been attracted by interpretative approaches like symbolic interactionism, phenomenology and ethno-methodology. Interactionism explores the ways in which human beings are constantly involved in negotiations with different social situations. The phenomenologist is essentially concerned with the regularities that may exist in individual perceptions and behaviour. We shall be examining this trend in the next chapter. Our present purpose is to concentrate on a sociological variation of what seems to be basically a Durkheimian offshoot- The Correspondence principle.

The Correspondence Principle

One significant sociological interpretation that explores the pedagogical situation, has come from the Neo-Marxist criticism. According to this, the school is a correspondent in society's plot to maintain inequalities. Both the Rationalist model of curriculum that underpinned the behaviourist school and the Process model advocated by the Progressivists fail to relate to the historical processes that mould man's reality. While the former reduces man to accommodate him to input-output theories, the latter magnifies his stature in a social vacuum. In so doing, both the perspectives make for abstract and idealized versions of both man and the larger framework in which he operates: society.

Traditional education in most universities, critics argue, has unquestionably an ideological stand that supports the existing social structures. In so doing, it has like its social counterpart strengthened the inequalities and the biases that are inherent in the school set-up. The school, then, had a deterministic quality which tamed the students into docility and conformity.

In questioning this compliance one becomes conscious of the pervasive nature of the ideology, the hegemony of a dominant group which serves its own interests at the expense of others. This dominant group, characteristically composed of the middle class, who posited the school as an agency of the state, promoted its own definitions of culture and intelligence. Within such a framework, only the middle class pupil will be successful, for only he can be successful. The others are either marginally successful or failures who are cut out for the lower rungs of societal functions. Thus, there seems to be a nurturing at the very sources to pattern out people to fit the division of labour in society.

Apple: Ideology and Curriculum

As Apple (1979) observes, the pervasiveness of the school ideology, which corresponded to the social structure was strengthened by the scientific temper and industrialization. Analytic competence that the Progressivists sought was a quality to be found only in the select middle class. Hence, it was this pupil over and against others who was the potential power-wielder.

According to Apple, systems appropriate to self-contained set ups like the management systems, were imposed on to the educational enterprise in an attempt to justify its logical operations. Evaluation, very importantly, came to mean accountability to a social stratum and its progeny, the school.

Selective Streaming

Basically, a system like this, based as it is on a set social pattern, supports only one group of individuals, the one which is powerful. The system ignores the less powerful or adjusts them to fit into the lower rungs of the industry. By catering to a select section of society, the middle class, it selectively screens out others in a hierarchy of vertical relationships. It is only as the Marxists set the Progressive curriculum in the historical perspective that the processes are understood as selective screening mechanisms providing for one kind of group, as against the others. In other words, the Neo-Marxists question the *givenness* of the curriculum by locating it in a historical perspective.

Curriculum, Apple argues, is the consensual agreement between society and school (interestingly, yet, ironically echoing Dewey) strengthened by the imposition of logical systems which provided justification in terms of productivity.

The unproductive elements are filtered out through various testing procedures to fit into more docile positions of society. From this perspective, Dewey's democratic ideal of education that make the child socially amenable is really a device that promotes the intelligent middle class child, familiar with the culture of the school. The primitive societies have nothing to contribute to such a curriculum. The primitive child, or a child from unschooled societies, as Bruner says, is context tied, or in Bernstein's (1975) words, his code is restricted as opposed to the universal or elaborated code of the middle class pupil.

Apple (1980) regards the manner of distributing high status curricular knowledge as a core element of the hidden curriculum of reproduction. Within a capitalist economy he claims "what is actually required is not the widespread distribution of high status knowledge to the populace in general but rather the maximization of its production". Consequently, according to him, low achievements are tolerated as they are of less consequence to the economy than is the generation of knowledge itself. The exclusion of these low achievers is made possible by the school's technical character. The class-biased nature of the school curricula, therefore makes it a device of filter for economic stratification. Schools, Apple observes systematically distort the function of social conflict.

The deterministic view is significant of Apple's early works which include predominantly his *Ideology and Curriculum*. His later works, however are characterized by an emphasis on the *relative* autonomy of the school system, where Apple describes reproduction a a process of contradiction and mediation. Pupils, he holds, engage in informal resistances to the school system, yet this resistance is contradictory, as it results in both partial penetration of the system on the one hand, and reproduction of the existing class relations on the other.

Curricula Operation

Explaining the mode of curriculum control operations, Apple observes, that forms of control are varied; the less obvious they are, the more powerful the hegemony of the dominating group. Power is made invisible through weaning it into the very structure of the work. The controls must come from the legitimized structure rather than from features like favouritism and so on which are obvious. It comes from the actual work itself. Definitions of curriculum come from the hierarchical structure of authority. This systematized control normally entails technical development.

Deskilling

Such technical control implies deskilling. Skills that the teacher used to need, such as deliberation and planning, are deemed as no longer necessary. It is only the execution of the processes that are carried out by the teacher. The planning is done at the level of production of both the rules for use of material and the material itself. In this process, valuable skills, says Apple slowly atrophy. The democratization of the process is underpinned by the dictates of methodology. A corresponding technical procedure requires the teachers to be reskilled for better controlling students and the teacher becomes something of a manager. Yet, as Apple and others later acknowledge, schools are different from factories in so far as (a) their products (labour) is not visible until later and (b) there are students who act back as no automobile on an assembly line can.

The Possessive Individual

Apple elaborates that the ideology in school is permeated as a subjectivity. This subjectivity, he notes, is an interesting shift from an ideology of individual autonomy where a person is his/her own boss to a careerist individualism. The rate at which one works may be individualized but the final product specifications, which the student never gets to see in school is pre-specified. Like one who accumulates wealth, the pupils accumulates skills all in bits and pieces. This is the possessive individual, of the lower classes.

Surrounded by such logic of control, resistances become difficult. Despite this, resistances are generated, more so within the relatively autonomous realms of the school. But whether these resistances are in themselves contradictory and continue to nourish the hegemonic set up or whether they have in themselves the potential for change, is yet to be explored.

Bowles and Gintis: On the Liberal Misconception

What dominated the Neo-marxist criticism for a long time was the correspondence principle although later works made significant modifications to the interpretation as we noticed in the work of Apple. The correspondence thesis was the main tenet in Bowles and Gintis's *Schooling in Capitalist America.* According to them, three basic goals underpinned the traditional liberal concept of the social code of schooling; (1) Education should be egalitarian in the sense of acting as an effective force for overcoming the natural inequities. (2) It should be developmental in so far as it should provide students with the means to develop the cognitive physical and emotional powers. (3) Education should be a means to what Dewey refers to as the 'social continuity of life' which promotes the smooth integration of individuals as members of society. Yet, what in fact, happens as Bowles and Gintis argue is that (in what seems a total reversal (is it?) of the liberal conception) education in advanced capitalism actually reproduced social inequality, and acted more as a repressive force rather than fostering personal development. Through these reversals, the schools produce the good citizen that the liberals sought.

Structural Correspondence

The critical problem, Bowles and Gintis (1980) argue, lies in the structural correspondence between the social relations of school life and the social relations of production. Schools, they assert, reproduce the existing social relations of capitalist society by reproducing the consciousness necessary for such relations. Given the undemocratic value of economic life, schools cannot fulfill their egalitarian and developmental objectives. The only means of achieving Progressive educational reform, to attain their objective is the democratisation of economic life, allowing for a democratic school system which does not conflict with the formation of adults capable of effective participation in the system of production. Failing that, education prepares students to fit into the vertical hierarchy of relationships in society. Like the division of labour in the capitalist enterprise, the educational system is a hierarchy of authority and control relationship where competition rather than co-operation holds sway.

This is the reason why the schools cannot at the same time promote full personal development and social equality, while integrating students into society. The authors observe that the hierarchical order of the school system, geared towards preparing students for their future positions in the hierarchy of production, limits the development of those personal qualities like free participation and reinforces social inequality by legitimating the assignment of students to inherently unequal 'slots' in the social hierarchy.

The Necessity of Economic Transformation

The Correspondence principle has important contributions to make. It makes clear the fact that egalitarian and humanistic education are unattainable not due to some inherent defect in human nature or the complexity of industrial society, but due to the undemocratic participation in economic life. For education to actually bring about the equality that Dewey visualizes and the personal development that such equality fosters, it requires "economic transformation towards democratic socialism". The Correspondence principle further stresses that it is not so much private ownership in a capitalism, but control that is central to social inequities. Merely passing from private to social ownership, without in any way disturbing the socio-economic relations, cannot lead to the humanistic goals of Progressive educational reform.

Invisible Pedagogies

Such a set up, which virtually posits education as a means to social equality covertly sets up a complex relations of structure which makes 'invisible' the control that is meted out to maintain the inequities intact. As we shall see, both Bernstein and Bourdieu arguing from the sociological perspective observe that the school is in fact a conservative institution which keeps intact inherent inequalities through its structural correspondence to the society at large.

Limitations of the Correspondence Principle: The Deterministic Stance

Yet, as it has been admitted by most critics, Bowles and Gintis too, confess that the Correspondence principle is beset with problems. They acknowledge that it is open to criticism in that it represents the relation between education and economy as a mostly harmonious one. The correspondence principle does not account for the contradictions that undoubtedly exist within the school. It is these contradictions which threaten the legitimacy of the predominant structure of social and economic relations. In the paper "Contradiction and Reproduction in Educational Theory", the authors offer a framework for coping with the capacity schooling has to reproduce social relations which both legitimate and contradict the existing ideological conditions.

Contradictions in the Liberal Discourse: Scope for Change

In attempting to trace these contradictions, Bowles and Gintis refer to three main structures; the state, family and capital production, which are basically three major relations that individuals have with society. Each of these is independently capable of supporting relations of dominance and subordinancy. The site of capitalist production can be characterized as the site of dominance of capital over labour and the family as the site of dominance of men over women. By contrast, the state in its liberal democratic form, while required to reproduce the condition of domination and sub-ordinacy in family and economy is not itself necessarily a site of domination.

Each of these sites articulates the appropriative political, cultural and distribution practices occurring within it. The particular nature of these sites in a capitalist society brings forth a totality that is contradictory in nature. The interaction between these sites may be characterized, according to Bowles and Gintis, as basically composed of two features: delimitation and transportation. Delimitation refers to the internal constraints within a site while transportation refers to the fact that under specific circumstances these sites attempt to transport features characteristic of other sites. For example, the funding of an educational system depends on its ability to enhance the economic status of its graduates. Thus the requirements for economic success determined within the frame of capitalist production structurally delimit the forms of change open to the educational systems, irrespective of the desires of the educational reformers. Conversely, educators intent on bringing about changes consciously transport political practices from the site of capitalist production to restructure the social relations of education. Rather than exhibiting a uniform set of social relations the peculiarity of schools lies in that they exhibit features of the state as well as of the private economy.

The state is organized according to the principle of majority rule, while the schools are structured on a basis of top-down control. This strategy does not make allowances for liberal policies that occur in the political set up of the state. To do so would not be compatible with their future position as workers. In addition, educators have drawn on the literature of business organization to mould the school into forms favourable for capital accumulation and subordination of the workers. These are examples of reproduction and transportation.

One may also speak of these mechanisms as contradictory. The critical location of the school with in the state makes it seem a democratic institutions, yet serves the site of capitalist production. Similarly the formally equal status of women as citizens gained in the early 20th century virtually ensures equal education to men and women. Yet the reproduction of hierarchical relations in the capitalist enterprise has depended on the subordination of women to men in the economy.

Therefore, the liberal concept of equality is manifestly unrealizable within the context of the capitalist class structure. This contradiction is clearly expressed in the person-property dichotomy. Education, in the capitalist enterprise reproduces rights vested in property while itself organized in terms of the rights vested in persons. It is therefore in the form of educational encounter in the social relations of education that accounts for its capacity both to reproduce capitalist relations of production and inability to promote healthy personal development. This is in fact a reflection of the *stress* in liberal discourse of procedure over substance.

Yet, this very discourse provides the tools by which it can be transformed into an instrument in the transition to socialism. The goals of progressive educational reform can be expressed as (1) the democratization of the social relation of education, effective only when the workers are in full control of the production processes. (2) Reformulation of the issue of democracy in curriculum which is articulated as a move towards teachers' and parents' control of the educational process. Liberalism, say Bowles and Gintis, puts forth a promise it cannot make good. The promise of equality, democracy and personal fulfillment, within the context of capitalism is empty. Socialists have tried to expose it, but true socialism lies only in the realization of the liberal promise and the transformation of the tools of discourse of capitalism.

Post Marxist Criticism

Despite the historical origins, which the Neo-Marxists draw on, they seemed to have, says Lynch, (1989), overlooked the universalysing features of the school which interface with the particularistic. It is in this interplay between the two that schools, says Lynch, are successful, in promoting the particular interests. The Neo-Marxists, according to her, have also underplayed the cultural contradictions inherent in the system. Yet another feature, which did not receive any attention in the Neo-marxist criticism is, as she points out, the predominant roles played by mediators like churches, administrators and so on in perpetuating these inequalities.

Lynch gives the example of post-colonial Ireland, where education is crucial to the attainment of wealth and power in a way it is not in the powerful industrialized economies. Hence, in addition to the economic contradictions that permeate the social relations within the schooling system, one needs to probe into the broader sociological perspectives to capture these contradictions in the liberal discourse.

Conclusion

In this chapter we have seen that the pedagogical and androgogical perspectives are limiting. To understand them in relation to Distance Education, it was suggested that it is necessary to probe into the sociological analysis. On a narrow level this analysis can be seen in the Correspondence Principle, which states that the school corresponds to the society in upholding inequalities. The next Chapter demonstrates the Correspondence Principle as it explores the Mainstream and Lower-stream curricula.

4

Main Stream vs. Low Stream Curricula: Setting Directions for the Distance Mode

In the previous chapter, the persistence of the Correspondence principle in curriculum organisation was discussed. It was suggested that the school corresponds to the society in maintaining and even promoting inequalities. This chapter, begins with a brief discussion of the question of power and the implications it has for the curriculum set up. In so far as one is powerful, this power not only gives one access to what is defined as the best of knowledge but also the power to decide what is good for others.

This chapter then discusses, the two streams of curricula; the one meant for the elite, the other for the masses. It goes on to present Bourdieu's analysis of the school as a conservative force, which while securing the interests of privileged few constantly reminds the low class pupil of his failure. The chapter then goes on to discuss Bantock's argument, who defends this differentiation. It then proceeds with a critique of streaming and a proposal for common curriculum, by virtue of both classes of people, having to live together in a single society with equality. Distance education, the chapter asserts, claiming to cater to the masses, has to make for a curriculum that in more ways than one compensates for the injustice meted out by the society. Therefore, the curriculum has to be so organized as to appeal both to the average learner and also to the bright one.

The emphasis, is then on distance education as an alternate mode of curriculum organization for all learners. Distance education does not assume any streaming trends. In so far as one calls it alternate, it alternates with the main stream mode. In this assertion, what, in fact, is established is the fact that it is not the curriculum differences, but the modes of teaching that alternate. Significantly, the emphasis is on a common curriculum where the Distance system would be a better mode to teach some skills and traditional mode better for others.

Selection Processes

Practically speaking, despite the fact that the school is a microcosm of society, it has to select suitable and manageable amounts of knowledge, skills and values for transmitting to the student. Notwithstanding the fact that these curricula are variously termed as open, child-centered and so on, the results ofselective processes are clearly visible in the classroom.

Essentially, the curriculum emerges as a result of compromises, negotiation and so on, but the underlying concept is that of power. It may be seen at two levels–first the power to take decisions that influence the work of students and teachers and secondly the control over the power that can be achieved by students or with held from them by determining access to high or low status curricular components and the evaluation and opportunities associated with them. Curriculum determination is unquestionably and even centrally concerned with both the use and the allocation of power. There are five key factors, says Eggleston (1977) that play a crucial role in curriculum making.

1. The definition of what is to be regarded as knowledge, understanding, values and skills.
2. The evaluation of this knowledge–into areas of greater or lesser important ones.

3. The principles of knowledge distribution; to whom and at what time various kinds of knowledge shall be made available and from whom they shall be withheld.
4. The identity of the groups whose definitions prevail in these matters.
5. The legitimacy of these groups to act in these ways.

High Status Curricula

The last aspect is of crucial importance as a curriculum exists and power distribution is real because people believe in the knowledge it contains and the justice with which it is distributed. It is possible to regard the curriculum as a collective representation of a community as indicated by Durkhiem. The process of determining the curriculum becomes, in other words, the process of social control. Questions such as 'who is chosen to experience different curricula' 'What parts of such curricula are available to different children?' become relevant in this context.

For quite sometime, formal education was generally only the experience of the small elite and was of a kind that enabled them to retain their status. Knowledge was defined by the vocational necessities of such groups. To those of humbler birth, development was predominantly provided by religious institutions like the Church, while the vast majority were simply ignored. Yet it was the elite curriculum that came to characterize the content of the curriculum until recently. The curriculum was essentially the Latin based classical curriculum, which was marked as high status knowledge. Marking of this knowledge made for a gentleman rather than a worker.

In Britain despite the industrialization in the wake of the 19th century, although the curriculum was broadened, it was basically based on Latin. The emergence of the public examination system developed the gradual process of selection based on educational achievement. This was basically to accommodate the rising middle class to various professional sectors of the industrialized society. In the latter half of the century, new groups with alternative definitions of knowledge emerged, who sought a dominant place for scientific knowledge.

Curriculum for the Masses

The curriculum of the school for the masses developed after the introduction of the compulsory schooling in 1870. This education was seen to be of a basically different kind, predominantly concerned with basic skills of numeracy and literacy. The content was basically different from the high status curricula, but what was significant was the fact that this curriculum was defined not by the consumers but by the same elite groups who defined high-status knowledge. It was defined in a way so as not to challenge the high-status curricula; it was meant to reinforce and re-emphasize the lower status of vocational and utilitarian knowledge and skills. An important characteristic of the new elementary school was that it should not give the poor ideas above their status.

It had other functions to perform besides providing minimal skills. Industrialization unsettled communities in the course of migration, which needed to be integrated. And the curriculum was a strong instrument through which the rule of law was established. Through this curriculum not simply knowledge and skills but values were transmitted. These values were defined as not only appropriate for life in man's society but also for the specific role and status for which the individual was destined. Similar processes are involved in the transmission of high-status curricula, as of low-status curricula the difference being only in content distribution. This difference stems from a definition and evaluation of knowledge that are common to both curricula. While the curriculum of the elite emphasized leadership, the curriculum of the elementary school stressed deference, submission and even servility. This distinction was supported by the prevailing belief in the possibility of reliable psychological differentiation of higher and lower ability children, for whom the grammar and the modern curricula respectively were suitable. The distinction became politically acceptable.

This differentiation not only made for a divisiveness, it also unified them in so far as it came to be accepted. One of the features of the mass curricula is to provide experience that emphasizes the student's incapacity and thereby further his acceptance of the legitimacy of different curricula for those who can. The curriculum brings a shared acceptance of social differences strongly reinforced by the administrative control systems of the social that legitimate differences in rank and status between individual children while still at school.

Cultural and Social Reproduction

The pedagogic work involved in schooling, claims Bourdieu (1974) is undertaken with a particular habitus, i.e., a system of schemes of thought, perception, appreciation and action which reflects the material and symbolic interests of the dominant groups. Bourdieu holds, that different social classes vary in their primary socialization, that is, life style of the family and the experiences it leads to. The habitus of working class life, therefore, is quite different from that of the middle and upper classes. It does not generate the cultural capital (knowledge) in the sense of the upper or middle classes) necessary for success in school. Neither do schools provide the means for appropriating it.

This leads the pupils to realize that their objective chances of success are low. Consequently, their aspirations are lowered. These low aspirations are nothing but objective chances intuitively perceived and gradually internalized.

The seemingly neutral position of the school coupled with the self-elimination of the majority of working-class grants the school legitimacy.

The school, says Bourdieu, is an effective means of perpetuating the existing social pattern as it both provides an apparent justification for social inequalities and gives recognition to the cultural heritage by treating a *social gift as a natural one*. The awareness of failure seems to be internalized by the pupil who fails. A circularity seems to be set up, as both the family and school reinforce this failure and discourage ambitions, to bring them down to reasonable hope or make them give up hope. Handicaps are thus cumulative. Given the equal achievement, the working class pupil is nevertheless directed to more general education while the others do the classics.

Similarly choices made at entry level dictate and influence future career prospects. Selection processes show that social advantages have been transformed into educational ones. Therefore, disadvantages linked with social class which dictate their first choice duplicate and reinforce their influence. The formal equity, says Bourdieu is in reality unjust and in any society which claims to have democratic ideals it protects the privileged rather than the underdog. By treating all people as equal, no matter how unequal they are, the educational system is led to give its *defacto sanction* to the perpetuation of cultural inequalities.

Justifying the Differentiation: Bantock

Such differentiation in curricula did not go unchallenged. Although differentiation existed, it was given psychological support as a difference that related to ability. If so, it required that the demonstrably more able be drawn into the upward stream. This was done, although it met with severe criticism. Critics like Bantock resented this mobility on grounds that it would lead to a dilution of standards. Such a mobility, according to Bantock (Entwistle: 1978) entails recruitment to upper classes of people lacking in traditional values. The author insists on close family ties on the grounds that social mobility, would be an intrusion into the institution of family. In support of this differentiation, Bantock (1975) calls for an education for the folk which would be affective–artistic as opposed to the cognitive intellectual that the humanists perfected. This culture is more oriented to the visual and the physical language of the body rather than to the development of the intellect. Bantock criticizes the move to extend schooling on the contention that for these pupils schooling has no value.

Bantock elaborates up on the Bernsteinian dichotomy between the restricted and the elaborated codes which refer to context tied and context detachable meanings respectively, a difference Burner recapitulates as one between the schooled and the unschooled. The abstract linguistic code of the school, says Bantock, is no place for the working class pupil. It makes for a cognitive development to which the working-class pupil cannot accommodate. He quotes the Piagetian experiment, as supportive of his argument, that in these people, cognitive development stops short at the concrete operations stage.

This research which concerned itself with distribution essentially sought its justification in psychology and left questions of knowledge definition and evaluation untouched. In so far as it did this, it contained the *conflict*. A similar conflict regarding the evaluation of low-status curricula which was mostly an *inside* debate retained a comparatively low profile. The relative failure of the various advocates of curriculum re-evaluation to bring about significant changes, says Eggleston, has largely been a consequence of their failure to achieve any substantial re-definition of high-status knowledge.

The most fundamental conflict, however is over the issue of the definition of knowledge. Outside the professional debate, the development of working-class education provided an equally consistent challenge to high-status definitions of knowledge. There were attempts to develop alternate definitions of knowledge that was at variance to the classical model. Efforts to achieve a distinctive and recognized section of knowledge enjoying the same status as the academic grammar school knowledge were continually put in. This was given due political support, but the effort was short-lived when the Progressive school began to make their impact. It is important, however, to see that these conflicts were not between elitism or egalitarianism as one between the identity and legitimacy of the contenders for memberships of the groups who define, evaluate and distribute knowledge and the power these confer.

The Case for a Common Curriculum: Entwistle, (1978)

The very fact that the elite as well as the working class live in the same society calls for some overlap, or a common base for interaction. According to Entwistle, (1978) over the wide range of every day activity, there is widely understood knowledge necessary for life in a community with individuals of differing interests. There is thus a large area of overlap representing the common culture. In this overlap two tendencies are predominant: Bourgeosification of the working class and Proletariatization of the middle class. The twin effects of affluence and technological change seem to make for a withering of the working class. With reference to the patterns of consumption, says Entwistle, it looks a if all are now middle-class. It is this sort of apparent identity of consumer habits across social class which probably account for American claims that the notion of a working class no longer has any relevance in the United States. Yet this assumption of working class burgeosification is questioned by sociologists who see no value shift beneath the veneer of affluence.

In Britain paradoxically, the withering of the working class is also implicit in the counter process, the proletarianization of the middle class through the tendency of the middle classes to assimilate the economic, political and educational institution of the Labour Movement. Proletarianization is also implicit in middle-class infiltration of the Labour Party and its participation in the Labour Party and its participation in the institution of the welfare-state. Through this process, the middle class also becomes the beneficiary of the welfare State provision. Indeed, it was Illich's assumption that the middle-class exploits public educational provision, at the expense of the poor that constituted his most congent advocacy of deschooling. This proletarianization of middle class could represent the working class's main contribution to the cultural mainstream.

It is imperative, therefore, by virtue of co-existing in a community that there be common curriculum regardless of the social divisiveness, at least in so far as it helps cope with the necessity of having to live together in a single community. If this is indispensable, it would be criminal to exclude the lower strata from access to knowledge. From the philosophical perspective, Hirst (1975) has already formulated the necessity of developing certain fundamental structures of knowledge to all. Appealing for a common curriculum, Entwistle criticizes Bantock's obvious attempts to throw the working class out of the cultural mainstream. He declares, that Bantock's unscrupulous attempt is to place the emotionally charged working groups at the mercy of the upper class intellect. Implicitly, he says, the appetites of the former must be in control. Without the cognitive capacities to make decisions, such control, must of necessity come from others. Bantock, Entwistle claims, ignores the political implications and the institutions like the Trade movement which have their origin in working class culture. According to Entwistle. Bantock trivializes working-class culture as *warmth and gregariousness* implying an inability to transcend limitations of place and time. Even appreciation of media, he feels, needs one to be politically and socially aware. "It is", he say "one thing to assert its existence (working-class culture) and another to reinforce such deprivation by provision of a cognitively reduced curriculum which Bantock proposes".

Questions relating to equality of opportunity, access and provision have been largely debated in view of the economic and the social disparity that such class divisions are inevitably associated with. For instance, *working* refers to the economic category, while *middle* refers to the social strata. Yet another point of controversy relates to the issue of equality of opportunity, where, it is not so much *equality* as *opportunity* that becomes crucial. It is the accessibility of opportunity rather than equality that matters.

Role of Distance Education

Distance education in pledging to serve the under-privileged needs to make significant curriculum decisions. It is as much to compensate for the past discrimination as to enrich the future.

The emphasis, throughout the thesis has been to study distance education and the possibilities it offers to operate as an *alternate mode* as different from an *alternative mode*. In other words, the attempt is to posit distance education as an alternate mainstream education and not as an alternative for the lower streams. It is crucial to conceive distance education not as continuing the process of streaming, which the correspondence principle seems to be suggesting, but as an alternate mode of organizing main-stream curriculum. The criteria therefore, on which distance education claims can be established is not to be based on the learner, but rather as the curriculum interests.

To elaborate, some learner needs could be best catered to through traditional face to face classes while others may function more appropriately, when distanced. Thus where distance education serves a primary role, traditional teaching could take on the supplementary role and vice versa. The idea of streaming of people, so to say, simply does not come into play. Rather that, it is envisaged as only one common curriculum which slips between the Distance Mode and the traditional teaching systems depending on the suitability of thc mode for the skill to developed.

Implications for ELT

Distance Systems, then, have to take account of those aspects of language learning which can reasonably be taught through its mode. Although thc second language status given to English makes it more of a language for functional purpose rather than for the richness of it, the fact that it is also a language, enables one to apprehend its richness. This move to study English as yet another language, also enables one to dissolve the discriminatory barriers between literature and language; where literature was until recently considered elitist as against the focus on language considered as mundane.

While English as an instrumental language was initially atleast upheld for its advantages, reaching upto the higher levels in the social hierarchy require more than this instrumentality. If one gives it the status of only a language, without attaching any value judgments, then English language learning becomes justified both on grounds of instrumental purposes as well as for literary appreciation. To the extent that the learner can see the similarities between the native language and the potential richness of English as a language, the sense of alienation can to a large part be overcome.

Such an appreciation that arises from the learner's sense of identification can contribute positively to language learning. An examination of the existing foundation courses in English (IGNOU & APOU) shows that language learning carries a functional perception on language which it is argued should not be the case in the Distance Mode. Skills of language learning and teaching are some aspects which need development by drawing on the learners's experiences. This in fact is the problem in face to face language teaching where simulations take the place of relevant real-life communications. A drawing on of real life learning experiences can in fact be best accomplished through the distance mode. This means perceiving language as richer than is seen in foundation course texts.

Conclusion

In this chapter, we looked at the two discrete streams of curriculum. The case for a common curriculum and the controversy that surrounds it were also discussed. A case for distance education was made, where it was stated that distance education is not an alternative curriculum for the lower stream pupils but an alternate organization of mainstream curriculum, so that parts of it could be made functional through distance, while others made useful through the face to face mode. Distance education is then projected as education, and not as mainstream and lower stream. It gets rid of the idea of 'streaming' which appears as a continuous, and sustained process as explored in the correspondence principle.

Significantly a language curriculum, is required that does away with the traditional distinction of literature and language, as it posits English as another language to be studied not just for instrumental purposes but its status as language.

5

Later Sociological Research: Reflexive Approaches to Curriculum Organization

The focus here is on the later sociological research, especially the phenomenological view of knowledge. It is argued here that knowledge is basically subjective which is posited as objective. To this extent, there is no quarrel with the Progressive stance. However, this subjective knowledge, it is asserted is also a social, and therefore human construct. It is precisely here that the sociological view deviates from the Progressive focus on the individual. Phenomenology looks at the individual as part of society, a facet which the Progressive over looked. While Breen and other process enthusiasts do speak of the classroom as a socio economic construct they do not look at the individual pupil's social background. Therefore, the possibility, that there are some meanings arising from the class that bypass the disadvantaged learner, is a fact that remains unacknowledged.

This chapter first looks at the phenomenology of knowledge as described by Berger and Luckmann. Through this analysis, the argument goes on to stress that different types of socialization at different stages, the primary and secondary and so on legitimize different kinds of knowledge patterns. Despite these differences, the writers assert, that there is a commonality by virtue of living together in a society. These common features hold the potential for retracing steps to make for a different kind of socialization; a different kind of legitimation. These social constructs appear inaccessible because, the legitimations become abstract, cut off as it were from the original base.

This realization that social constructs which appear objective can be subjectively experienced by people in different divisions of the society, enables one to become more reflexive, rather than take curriculum as *given or received.* From this perspective the Progressive stance can be interpreted as *received.* For Bruner, as for Hirst, knowledge structures or themes are already defined. They are given in one particular social framework. Yet the failure to give these definitions a definite social cast leads them to project this definition as universal. The phenomenological approach emphasizes the reflexive organization of curriculum, where it is possible to question knowledge forms, put them back in a given social setting, and then allow for choices.

Yet *scope* for such reflexiveness must take account of the larger curriculum set up. Therefore, despite the distance mode's commitment to individualization, especially with reference to objectives, pacing and so on, it cannot do away with some pre-specified rationales of the curriculum. To this extent while some objectives are set out, others are achieved in the *process* of learning. This reflective approach in organizing a curriculum allows for more flexibility where language learning is concerned. Of particular interest here are factors relating to the geographical status of the learner, the status of the language in a particular society and the resources available for promoting the language.

The Phenomenological Approach

Knowledge, say Berger and Luckmann, (1967) as man understands it, is a subjective experience that is objectively experienced as real. From the phenomenological point of view human consciousness is always intentional; it is directed towards objects. These objects form part of different realities. The everyday reality is experienced in different degrees of closeness and remoteness and is by nature intersubjective. This reality is routinized, yet appears problematic when juxtaposed with other realities. In a face to face situation intersubjective activities take place on a reciprocal basis. Such relationships although flexible, operate through certain typical procedures leading to a negotiation between participants. In remote situations, such typifications which are essentially predictions based on habit become more anonymous. Social structure is the sum total of these typifications and the recurrent patterns of interaction established by means of them.

Language Objectifies Reality

Language is a crucial part of this social structure which has its origins in the face-to-face situation, but which can do without it. It makes real one's own subjective experience in so far as it objectifies it. In its ability to detach itself from reality, it helps bridge the gap between various realities as also integrating one into a meaningful whole. Thus language helps in accumulating knowledge. By virtue of this accumulation, a social stock of knowledge is built up which is transmitted. Such accumulation is further selectively done. This knowledge, shared by others is constantly affected by common participation. This knowledge is more accessible to some in some areas and not accessible in others. Knowledge therefore, is encountered as a possession differently held by different people. The social distribution of knowledge which begins very simply culminates in very complex systems of expertise.

Man is World Open

Man's relationship to his environment is characterized by what the authors call 'world-openness'. Man's instincts are undirected as Dewey and Durkheim earlier noted. The direction takes place largely in interaction with the environment or society. Human plasticity is particularly obvious in that the way of becoming human are as numerous as man's cultures. Humanness is a socio-cultural variable. This social order is a necessity to provide direction for human activity.

Habitualization

A basic tenet to the formation of the social order is habitualization. Through this device, man provides a direction for his inner drives. Such processes of habitualization precede any institutionalization. Institutions are born of typification, and by their existence control human conditions by setting predefined patterns of control. In transmission, institutions are legitimated and possess an objective reality of their own. Ordinarily, institutionalization occurs in collectivities but it would occur when two individuals interact. Such institutions need to be legitimated for future generations who posit the problem of compliance. Social conduct becomes more controllable and predictable through institutional legitimation. Such legitimation is generally superimposed by a logical order which language provides.

Role Typologies

The construction of role typologies is a necessary correlate of institutionalization. By playing roles the individual participates in the social world. When these roles are internalized, they become subjectively real to him. To learn a role, one must be initiated into the various cognitive and affective aspects of the body of knowledge relevant to it. This implies a social distribution of knowledge which entails a dichotomy of knowledge in general and role-specific relevance. With the emergence of role-specific knowledge, levels of meaning are created and legitimated. Such legitimations often operate autonomously and act back on the stock of knowledge that initially produced it. The relationship between knowledge and its social base is a dialectical one; that is, knowledge is a social product and knowledge is a factor in social change.

Legitimations and Reifications

Legitimations, therefore, become indispensable in so far as they have to build boundaries where insiders need conviction and outsiders need to be eliminated. Then, there is the possibility for institutions to get reified; appearing as objects, and unreal, though it is human activity that produced them in the first place. Because, they are products of human activity, all social universes change and the change is brought about by the concrete action of human beings.

Curriculum as a Subjective Social Construct

From the phenomenological perspective, then, curriculum is a human construct, which is defined by the human entity. It can be redefined depending on the changing needs, as also from a different perspective. In this sense, no curriculum is absolute. It is relative to human perception. Yet, in so far as it remains stable, it is based on a regularized pattern of human behaviour if only for a certain period of time. In this sense, the curriculum of itself has no power structures except those that the human thrusts on it. In so far as the curriculum is institutionalized, it may exercise control, yet alternate legitimations born of different perceptions, can effectively remove such controls. Therefore, curriculum depends on a large extent on the processes of selection, distribution and evaluation, all societal processes which get legitimated.

Sociology and the Curriculum

The crucial question that has to be asked from a sociological perspective is what exactly is considered to be knowledge in a society, and what is non-knowledge. Differences in thought processes and differences in the perceptions of events lead to differences in the nature of knowledge possessed by each society and each group. These stores of knowledge transmitted from generation to generation with only gradual modifications form the culture of societies and groups.

Societies have procedures for transmission as well as internalization of this knowledge content. In pre-industrial society this function was usually assumed by the church community and family, while in industrial societies such socialization comes to be achieved through the *school* and its curriculum. In other words, schools become instruments of social control, as already suggested by the Correspondence principle and help ensure the maintenance of the social system its knowledge, its status, stratification and above all its power. Such knowledge is not simply defined, transmitted and legitimated, it is also distributed. Every society has selection procedures by which it distributes knowledge; and such knowledge is basically evaluated as high status or low status.

The school is, however, not an autonomous social institution. This is especially significant in relation to the power structure it formulates. The norms and power systems of the school either reflects what is acceptable to the society or else through its limited channels, challenges these social structures through a response that must still take account of them. The Curriculum of the school involves a pattern of learning experience that conforms to the social view of nature, distribution, and availability. Consequently, it is subject to change. The curriculum components like aims, methods, spring from the normative and power system of society. Significantly, it has a larger than life image something that can't be achieved fully.

The Hidden Curriculum

In reality, official curriculum statements often differ widely in practice. Such differences, visible in the 'hidden' curriculum often take the form of alternative orientation to the official knowledge, satisfying teacher's requirements, responding in ways acceptable to peers and teachers. It also includes knowledge of where cheating is tacitly approved. Response to the hidden curriculum is as important for the student's personal survival as to the official curriculum. 'Hidden' is here used not in the Neo-Marxist sense but as indicative of practices not acknowledged by the official curriculum. It may be of greater importance to the teacher as without it teachers have to work to rule, if students are not allowed to use mutual help.

In the Neo-Marxist sense, the hidden curriculum also helps some pupils to understand that they *cannot* learn maths and helps them to respect those who *can*. The Sociologist is concerned with the realities of social behaviour. Therefore, despite the official statements of the curriculum his interest centers on the practices which are defined differently.

Received Perspective

Curriculum varieties come under labels traditional, progressive, child-centered, teacher-centered and so on. Studies on these curricula usually provide the pupils with arguments to reinforce the present practices and identity. To proceed with the sociological analysis of any particular curriculum, one has to probe the underlying ideologies and the important implications of power that spring from them. Eggleston (1977) describes two particular forms of curriculum, one which is a broad term for the basic trends that are currently in practice, he terms as the received perspective.

According to Eggleston, it is one in which curriculum knowledge, like other components of the knowledge system in the social order, is accepted as a received body of understanding that is *given*, even ascribed, and is predominantly *non-negotiable*. It is essentially non-dialectic and consensual. In its fundamentals the perspective is received by the teacher and the pupils as part of a given order. There are, therefore, associated with it, established standards, norms of behaviour, rituals and hierarchical divisions.

Progressive Curriculum Redefined

The basic justification for the Received Perspective comes from philosophical and psychological resources. Therefore, accounts of the nature of knowledge led to discussions of categorization of knowledge. If, as they propose, knowledge consists of a limited number of forms that may be identified, then it offers the most crucial challenge to the definition, evaluation and distribution of knowledge.

Hirst, for example, speaks of forms of knowledge that arise from seven or eight distinguishable cognitive systems, as was earlier noted in Chapter One. These forms of knowledge have certain distinctive features. Curriculum can be described for Hirst in terms of the forms and the fields of knowledge and the formal structures like them. Although, he does not advocate a subject base curriculum, he does require that any curriculum must remain true to the underlying form of knowledge that it must include. The fundamental purpose of education is for him, the development of mind, by a conceptual distinction of these various forms. From a sociological perspective he ignores the social context in which these processes must occur. Curriculum objectives are determined by these forms of knowledge and the development of the pupil's mind. Thus, in short, though Hirst does not prescribe a curriculum as such, the moral imperatives of choosing an appropriate form of curriculum that helps develop the mind, are obvious. Hirst's position, as we have already seen, has been challenged in different ways by Bourdieu working from within the reflexive perspective and also by writers like Bantock who do not accept Hirst's view that there is 'no need for a radically new pattern of curricula or that the central objectives of education are the development of mind'.

The received curriculum gets further justification from psychological resources (despite the progressive move towards innovation, their basic failure to relate to a given social context also renders their definition of knowledge problematic). The prescriptive psychology of predictive testing and individual differences has clear implications for the distribution, evaluation and definition of the curriculum. The ability to identify and measure human capacities, led to Bloom's taxonomy of objectives on which the curriculum was based.

A more sophisticated argument emerges from the progressive desire for innovation. Although similar in intentions as Hirst, in so far as their processes lead to an inquiring mind, their methodological explorations are wide-ranging. For Bruner, structured fields of knowledge exist; learning for him depends on precisely apprehending these structures and the context within which they occur. He argues that skill transfer is impossible without access to such structures. A realization of these structural relationships also makes for economy and retention.

The reason for the inclusion of diverse writers like Hirst, Bruner and others under one perspective is that they operate from a common view that there are established and knowable structures of knowledge that exist independently of teacher or indeed of any other individuals, and that these patterns may be discovered, clarified and comprehended, and that adherence to them is either necessary or desirable if curriculum is to be meaningful and learning experiences successful.

Main Stream/Lower Stream Curricula Reinterpreted

A Social variation of the given definition of knowledge as exemplified in the Correspondence Principle is that knowledge is basically of two types, the high and the low, which we have already discussed. The occupational division that supports this makes it appropriate to think of low-intellect education for the masses involved in labour while high–intellect or superior knowledge for the elite. As we have seen Bantock provides a persuasive argument, appealing for a non-cognitive, emotion bound knowledge that appeals to the masses while the cognitive print-media is more in tune with the superior skills of the elite. Bantock's suggestions have been widely criticized on the grounds of deliberate differentiation between the academic minority and the non-academic masses. Entwistle (1978) for instance, feels that Bantock's differentiation is a deliberate attempt to place the masses in the control of a few.

Yet Bantock draws attention to a real problem in so far as he highlights the arbitrary nature of such knowledge divisions, with one getting a superior status and the other an inferior one. Hogart, (cited in Eggleston: 1977) for instance, feels that it is unlikely that the majority will take to intellectual pursuits. Yet there are, he feels, other ways of knowing the truth. Discussing the debate, Lawton argues "the problem in terms of curriculum is thus to find a way of bridging the gap between the academic and the every day and not to force half digested academic ideas down unwilling throats of all classes and all abilities". The solution, he feels, does not lie in dividing people neatly into two closed categories (Eggleston: 1977).

Reflexive Approach

The second perspective which Eggleston terms reflexive, is one in which curriculum knowledge, like the components of the knowledge system, is seen to be *negotiable*; in which content may be legitimately criticized and argued or new curricula devised. Essentially, it is dialectic and manifestly subject to political and other influence; a construction of those who participate in its determination. The two perspectives, namely, the Received and the Reflexive represent polar views on the nature of social control and the distribution of power in society.

Set against the received perspective we see the alternative in the reflexive perspective; that curriculum is an artifact constructed by teachers and others responsible for determining the experience of students. In some situations, students may also take part in such decision-making. Support for such a view stems from the striking changes that takes place in the definition of important areas of knowledge. Earlier definitions of 'maths' are different from the current ones. Similarly, emergence of new subject areas cast doubts on the ultimacy of curriculum knowledge. No curriculum, can be either totally absolute or wholly relative. It has necessarily to spring from a defined base, but is constantly redefined, (at least significant parts of it) as a result of human choices. These choices have significant sociological consequences. Inevitably, the reflexive perspective finds support in sociologists–such as Marx, Mannheim and Young.

Marx (Eggleston: 1977)

Much of the dynamic of the reflexive perspective still derives from the ideas of Marx. Though in no way specifically concerned with formal educational arrangements, his analysis saw societies as characterized by ruling class determination of the definition, evaluation and distribution of knowledge, a definition, established through the control of the economic system. For Marx, the situation is not a given one; through an identification of the culture of the working culture and a revolutionary challenge to the ruling class culture, a new egalitarian culture could prevail.

Mannheim (Eggleston: 1977)

Mannheim more definitely focused on the nature of knowledge and the social processes associated with its establishment and continuance. Thus in Mannheim's assertion that "...mental structures are inevitably differently formed in different social and historical settings", we already see the articulation of the reflexive perspective. His assertion that social backgrounds of human groups with distinctive perspectives ensure differentiated groups, suggest limited views of reality rather than universal ones. Such relative perceptions, according to Mannheim, accounted for the greater part of human knowledge, though he specifically excluded mathematics and some aspects of science from his thesis.

Like Marx, Mannheim believed that it was possible for individuals to modify their view of reality. Through conscious efforts or appropriate guidance they may come to perceive reality from different perspectives without necessarily being constrained by their original ones. The way to do this is through detachment from class involvement, typical of the scientific aspirations. Yet that 'Science' itself is 'value-free' is again a dubious presumption as was noted in the previous chapter. (See also Ramphal: 1992).

In refusing to acknowledge this position, Mannheim avoids the extreme relative version of the reflexive perspective.

Young (Eggleston: 1977)

Young's analysis of curriculum develops on five levels described by Lawton. They are:

(1) It concerns itself with the social distribution of knowledge.
(2) With what counts as knowledge in our society and the stratification of knowledge.
(3) Subject barriers are arbitrary; in control of those in power.
(4) All knowledge is socially constructed.
(5) That not only knowledge but that rationality itself is merely a convention.

The interpretative paradigm that Young formulates clearly raises questions on the nature and practice of the received curriculum and in itself makes for a compelling self-justification. Why, for example, Young asks do we still continue to provide a curriculum at which working-class children regularly and predictably fail? Why are subjects divided as high status and low status? Why do working class almost always choose low-status subjects? These arguments undoubtedly bring to light the persistent strength of the received perspective in the school curriculum and the persistence of elitist orientations in the determination evaluation and distribution of knowledge.

The Need for a Restructuring Perspective

Yet both these perspectives i.e. the received as well as the reflexive are incomplete in themselves. On the one hand the received perspective fails to account for the deviations from the given forms and distribution of knowledge. On the other hand, the reflexive paradigm cannot account for the visible regularities that occur in the individuals construction of reality. If not for these, societies would simply vanish. This is not to say that such patterns do not change. Kuhn points out that even in science, patterns of knowledge, usually taken as *objective 'facts'* change. New authorities many emerge to provide solutions for problems that could not be solved in the existing pattern. If successful, then the field may be restructured around them.

It is always a restructuring in which much of previous pattern is retained, and not as if the entire pattern is demolished. This is partly accountable for the power structures established by the pattern. The situation corresponds to that of schooling in which a deviant is often punished in various ways. In so far as the pattern continues to hold powerful these are internalized by all, so that they do not need to be constantly made aware of the constraints. For the average teacher, reality is far removed from both perspectives. In the extreme, they are not likely to demonstrate that reality is other than as he experiences it. But at a modest level, they have something useful to offer. They encourage him to ask why things are as they are, the social significance of his time-table and so on.

Therefore, to emphasize on one at the expense of the other perspective is to do a disservice, since the curriculum is built on both these perspectives. Eggleston, brings them together through a third perspective, what he calls the *restructuring perspective*. As two modes of understanding, the two perspectives describe the realities of knowledge within the school curriculum and the possibilities of change therein. If the received perspective shows the way in which curriculum knowledge as defined and evaluated by the teacher are of crucial importance to the achievement of the child, then the reflexive perspective, shows that the achievement and life chances are themselves socially determined categories. This new emphasis takes the argument well beyond the middle-class/working class dissonance. Becker (Eggleston: 1977) has demonstrated that at least in theory, any category of student can be defined as disadvantaged from what the prevailing view of knowledge of the teacher happens to be.

The potential of the restructuring perspective is considerable. It has obvious use in examining the assumptions of both the received and the reflexive perspectives underlying curriculum. It offers the opportunity to look at components like teacher behaviour and the concept of power, hitherto underplayed in both perspectives. The advantage of the restructuring perspective stems neither from the received nor from the reflexive thesis but from history.

Implication for ELT

In terms of language teaching, Curriculum, traditionally, was seen as given. Thus, the banking concept was as much part of the Behaviourist store of knowledge; whether in terms of grammatical structures or functional notional categories. It was information to be accumulated for future use. A similar concept of language is seen in Bruner's knowledge structures or even in Hirst's forms of knowledge which are essentially static. This is inevitable in so far as it is born of a deliberate attempt to keep control in the hands of a few. Thus as Bernstein analyses 'process' elements in what he calls the integrated codes, he remarks that the apparent democratic tendencies only support the existing power structures more strongly by rendering pedagogical structures invisible.

The 'static' conception of language becomes very obvious in what Bernstein refers to as collected codes. Here the organizational rigidity is visible to the pupil. Although Bernstein makes no reference to the functioning of the language curriculum, it is easy to illustrate his conceptions through the description he gives of the pedagogical structures. Thus, the visible and static language curriculum of the collected codes is rendered invisible in the integrated codes, although, *the essential static nature of the language curriculum is kept intact.* This is precisely why mainstream education fails, especially in promoting language learning successfully. Despite the considerable number of years spent in this effort, language learning in particular seems to escape its grasp.

Distance Systems, it appears begin to function where mainstream education gives up. Operating through prespecifying objectives and prespecifying the subject matter to be learnt, Mainstream Education ceases to furnish any new perspectives. The end seems inevitable in the beginning. It is here that the Distance Mode reaches out to open new fields of experiential reality. It renders problematic the givenness, both of the knowledge content of the learner and the new resources of learning towards which the learner progress. It makes one reflects upon his/her own resources of knowledge and allows for a restructuring perspective.

This reflective approach, characteristic of contemporary ELT methodology owes its origin to the social scientist's subjective rendering of what appears to be objective truth. This reflexiveness is significantly different from both the scientific model that Bloom designed, or the individualized version of the Progressive school. This new orientation makes possible the emergence of a new language so to speak, that strikes roots in the Indianized version of English. To this extent, it is quite possible that some of the features of the local languages might penetrate into English as well.

English language curriculum then becomes a dynamic and exploratory field which refuses to accept any given model of language. In so far as there are a multiple range of languages, multiple varieties of the English language are possible, with a common base. The multiplicity also increases when we take into account the individual differences of each of these learners. Basically catering to the adult, the Distance Mode necessarily has to take into consideration factors as the native language competence, occupational diversity and leave the options open to the learner. The curriculum, then, has to necessarily take the social aspects of the learner in order to set up a curricular theme. It is to this social construction of the curriculum that we must now look to enable us to explore the definition, distribution and evaluation of the language curriculum.

Conclusion

In this chapter, we looked at the reflexive trends in sociology and the positive implications they have for the distant mode of education. In terms of the Distance Education curriculum this reflexiveness necessitates a probing into the historical perspective, as also calling for remoulding the curriculum to allow for the learner growth. For language in particular, this approach appeals not just to the psychological aspects of the learner but also to his social definitions.

6

Opening Ways for a Possible Restructuring of Knowledge/Curriculum

This chapter examines how distance education systems have made ample space for the reflexive perspective, and allow for the necessary restructuring. In particular, it explores the British Open University programme in order to study in depth the notions of adult education. The concept of openness, the interdisciplinary nature of the curriculum, the use of multi-media, the predominance of print and other such issues crucial to the functioning of the open university are also discussed to demonstrate possibilities for restructuring Curricula against the rigid structures of the traditional face to face programmes.

The chapter also discusses such controversial issues as autonomy and control and finally it explores the, possibility of redefining process elements as they were studied in the Progressive curricula, and argues that the distance mode provides for a suitable framework within which these elements can be realised. Finally it suggests that while its contribution to pedagogy remains doubtful, within the realm of adult education, the distance mode seems to offer the best possible and a working curriculum. In terms of language learning too, the Distance Mode implies positive connotations.

The chapter focusses on the adult as a person with a definite socio-economic background. Given that the student in the distance mode of education is an adult working in the socialized institutions of labour, the kind of education that he receives should be, it is generally acknowledged now, qualitatively different from what the student receives in the pedagogical institution of the school.

Assuming that there are processes of socialization that operate at the level of knowledge and in the form of institution both of education and occupation, the adult that one has to deal with is an already socialized being; socialized primarily into a given system of knowledge as also the occupational institution where he works, which in Berger and Luckman's analysis is the secondary process of socialization, with its own processes of legitimation.

While the primary socialization remains closer to the 'adult' it is the secondary socialization that presently occupies him. To the extent that primary socialization is reinforced by the school, (the adult is more firmly tied to his occupational status) the lower class-child's natural and limited cognitive powers are strengthened. Yet, if one gives the 'school' the benefit of doubt by appealing to its potential for change, this could have made for a different kind of socialization. Whatever may have been the outcomes of schooling we have to now deal with the adult with a definite socio-economic function in society. It is with this adult in mind that we shall explore the curriculum possibilities that the distance mode promises.

Adult Education: Emerging Paradigms

Adult education theorists as was pointed out earlier, have so far explored curriculum models predicated upon an apolitical concept of knowledge. Other views relate to a view of knowledge in a context of inevitable change; change running out of human control and knowledge exploding without apparent reference to the social cultural and political condition in which it is created. Therefore, despite the theoretical distancing of adult education from schooling and the innovative characteristics of adult education, in terms of knowledge, adult education tends to reproduce the curriculum categories of traditional Progressive schooling. This is bound to happen in so far as they fail to underpin their claims to democratization, egalitarianism and popular control with a transformational analysis of the knowledge content itself.

Writers such as Illich, Freire and Gelpi have attempted in different ways to conduct a new paradigm and to engage in such a transformational analysis of knowledge. All the three writers have demonstrated in different degrees, the ways in which institutions give expression to the political construction of knowledge and as such constitute obstacles to the transformation of knowledge. It is not necessary to associate institutionalization with repression; but it is necessary according to them to understand education as much in terms of the politics of knowledge as of the politics of the educational institution.

There is now the tendency to think of the childhood/adult-hood distinction as political categories. There is a sense in which this distinction is an institutionalized invention of education systems reflecting all the socio-historical conditions that relate to culture, class, family, work and so on. The need for a critical historical perspective on the social construction of knowledge is, therefore, crucial.

Illich, Freire and Gelpi seem to be engaged in the task of rediscovery; a rediscovery that implies a political analysis of knowledge. This kind of analysis stands in contrast to adult education theory which focuses consistently upon the distinction of adulthood as a learning category or upon the nature of provision appropriate to such a category and upon the liberal view of knowledge as that which transcends politics.

Illich, Freire and Gelpi, reject the ideology of needs, access and provision in favour of a much more political view of knowledge and are skeptical of the institutionalized apparatus of learning to which in the end, the ideology of needs has a direct reference.

Illich: Deschooling Society

Illich talks of Deschooling not only education but society itself, using the school as his paradigm. "Not only education but social reality itself has become schooled" says Illich (Cited in Griffin: 1983). The author shows how childhood would go out of production if there were no age specific and obligatory learning institutions. The school casts the teacher in a repressive role, as it also progressively creates need and makes for a kind of consumerism. Adult education, for Illich, gives rise to a similar kind of consumerism. Learning for Illich, is a personal activity and can only be determined in personal terms.

Paradoxically, as we see, although Illich sees schools as political institutions, his view of knowledge is strangely unproblematic. He provides little sense of the fact that knowledge is itself full of contradictions or itself a kind of manipulated institution. The deschooled society that he speaks of, deliberately avoids the issue of the content of knowledge in favour of a suitable methodology of learning. As Gintis observes, (Cited in Griffin: 1983) the trouble with the deschooling thesis is that it is an idea constructed exclusively around that of consumption. In so doing, Illich, in fact treats as *pathological*, the *normal* institutional conditions of capitalism. He does not provide the kind of ideological analysis of knowledge that is necessary to think of adult education either in terms of curriculum reproduction of schooling or of transformation of knowledge content.

Freire: Resolving the Teacher-Learner Contradiction

With Freire, (1983) the argument moves a little further. His account of culture, education, and revolution is informed by Hegelian dialectics and existential authenticity. Teaching and learning for Freire, are in dialectical contradiction and it is in resolving this contradiction that another education must begin. The idea of banking education described the inauthenticity of schooling; its apparent incapacity to resolve the contradiction that lies at the heart of the educational enterprise. And it so far as the adult curriculum reproduces that of the school many ideas of adult education are really in Freire's terms inauthentic. Freire is clearly concerned with the social relations of education and the way in which they express the contradiction of teaching and learning. However, he has not much to say on the content of learning, itself. There is obviously some relationship between the construction of knowledge and the teaching/learning contradiction, but Freire does not enter the issue deeply. Like Illich, Freire's idea gives in to a more methodological orientation and only indirectly relates to the problem of knowledge as a social construction.

In the social and political contexts with which Freire and Illich were concerned, consumerism and oppression create a kind of universal dependence in which the distinction between childhood and adulthood is of little significance. Who grows to adulthood in such conditions? While both Freire and Illich provide negative critiques of schooling, their analysis of the social construction of knowledge remains curiously unproblematic. It is to Gelpi we look for a formulation of knowledge as it appears 'problematic'.

Gelpi: Towards an Authentic Adult Education Programme

Gelpi's analises the contradiction identified by Freire as an expression of the social relation of production. But unlike Illich, for him this is a *normal* not a *pathological* condition of certain societies in certain historical conditions. Gelpi locates the problem of adult education in a comparative and international perspective and relates it the problem of the division of labour in society, which ultimately sets the terms for a discussion of educational concepts.

Gelpi's view of adult education is dialectical and accounts for both reproduction and the transformational potential for adult-education. The possibility of transformation exists for Gelpi by a process characterized by relative autonomy, even though absolute autonomy in prevailing social forces is out of question. The policy of adult education depends much more on the analysis of the division of labour in society, the social relation of production which express this division and the processes by which the curriculum categories of educational institutions reproduce or transform the social distribution of knowledge. Educational theorizing and planning, he feels tends to be divorced from the cultural social and political factors which in the end largely determine what happens.

Against Progressivism

Progressive educators says Gelpi, have failed to take account of the world of production which is so significant for personal and social development. It is the division of labour rather than the modernization process which makes adult education relevant. The real relationship between education and work cannot be grasped in pedagogical terms. Education, says, Gelpi, can be linked to cultural, social and economic transformation on condition that it is based on social forces and not on structures. This is of special significance to adult education which is often at variance with the established structures. A traditional preoccupation with these structures of provision has only resulted in a reproduction of the school curriculum. Gelpi makes a distinction between knowledge for application to the material world and knowledge as structured in the relations of production. The latter is as important as the former. The educational requirements of the workers, says Gelpi must be based on different assumptions: different from the knowledge categories of schooling. The democratization of knowledge has important implications for professionalism and the structure of education since, "hierarchical relationships cannot be allowed to perpetuate the cultural dependence of adults on educational institutions".

Whether education is sought by adults for its intrinsic value or as a response to the logic or production is a duality, which Gelpi says, paralyzes educational debate. Motivation for adults, thc author claims is most genuine when it arises from a wish to improve their living conditions and especially to take part in the management of their society. These motivations are often ignored by educational institutions which prefer to induce adults to adapt themselves to the needs of production or to engage in cultural or educational activities as a response to the alienation resulting from their work. All too often needs are predicated upon some professional criteria, whereas adult learning activities require, says Gelpi, that the contents and methods of education are brought into discussion. Workers, he says are not enhanced by admission to a culture and an education in which they have no control of objectives method or content. Similarly, their needs could not be identified on these terms either.

Role of Family

Gelpi attributes a crucial role to the family, despite the fact that the relations between educational and family structures tend to reinforce institutional roles. The family, says Gelpi, gives expression to the culture of a great majority of persons and when this culture is recognized as an educational force, workers can be teachers and not merely "adult students". A new relationship says Gelpi, between work and education is no longer a question of the access of workers to the educational institution but is rather the presence of workers as educators within their structures. Gelpi sees the relationship of work and education most fundamentally as an issue of the social construction of knowledge.

Redefining and Restructuring Curricular Issues: The British Open University

In calling for this kind of a student to be on its rolls, and in promising to provide for the kind of education that enables the adult to make for a resocialization into other societal divisions and institutions, and thus create opportunities in the true spirit of democratization, the Distance System has to necessarily make its structures flexible and open; open to people, places, methods and ideas.

The Concept of Openness

The Distance mode makes no arbitrary gradation from one level to other levels by which the traditional universities establish their criteria for admission. There are no formal entrance qualifications. It enables thousands of people who for one reason or other did not get the opportunity to educate themselves. The existing system leaves unrecognized a great reservoir of human talent and potential, that the distance Mode attempts to bring into its preview.

It is open to places. It virtually has no walls in the sense of a closed classroom or even a building where people are expected to come and knock at its doors. It is spread all over, precisely because it does not locate itself in any one place. It goes to people and therefore makes itself accessible. It uses the technological revolution to its full in exploiting the media widely. Every new form of communication is used to raise human understanding. The distance mode also claims that it is open to ideas. It accepts both the traditional form of learning, advocated by the structuralists as also the innovative and more democratic strategies that includes the *learning to learn* kind of possibilities. Only by so doing it can keep itself open to the varied student qualities that it has to cater to.

Interdisciplinary Curriculum

One of the most interesting features of the Open University has been the interaction of the academics with one another in an effort to break the socialization caused by occupational divisions. It breaks the traditional barriers between disciplines and makes for a kind of despecialization that has its own sociological consequences. Legitimations are no longer the privilege of the specialist. They need a broader base to provide them with a *rationale*. The networks of relationship between subjects had to be established and this called for a lot of discussion among the various academicians. Common trends as also different ones had to be worked out. This was crucial for methodological purposes both in learning and teaching. This interdisciplinary approach is significant in the face of the traditional main stream tendency, to ceil subject boundaries, to keep away intruders. For now, we are caught by the *idea* rather than the discipline itself. In other words, the search for intersection common patterns demands a dissolution of distinctions. This has implication for occupational diversity and the possibilities of breaking down or atleast making one aware of the probability of reaching out to other areas of socialization.

The interdisciplinary nature of the Distance Mode, must seek its justification not through the elitist tradition but to the understanding of the average learning public to whom it is ultimately responsible. It therefore cannot be the classics or the watered down version of the classics but a curriculum that partakes of all relationships across subject boundary socialization in an attempt to resocialize into a true democratic mould.

Yet this very 'democratic mould' can be institutionalized into a kind of rigid structure that denies its own origins. This is precisely the aspect on which Norman Birn Baum (Turnstall/ed 1974) warns us. There is, says Birnbaum, every danger of this Open Mode becoming centrifugal.

The Use of the Television

The aura of the specialized subject areas is really an illusion that the Distance Mode demystifies. Through its exploitation of the media and use of the most non-formal techniques, it accesses even the most specialized areas in a simple and unobtrusive manner. The Home experiment Kits enable students to do their experiments at home without necessitating his/her presence at the respective institutes. The demonstration experiments shown through the T.V. give a close-up view of the processes not possible in an overcrowded class room. The T.V. also provides for more than lectures. It exposes us to the critical comment that has so far remained unpublished. Since a T.V. programme is deliberately planned and produced with the best communicators that it can draw, it does away with the possible irresponsible nuances of a formal lecture. The television in addition, can also link abstract mathematical to real life situations. Animated graphics make for superb teaching aids, especially for the average learner.

The Personal Element in the Material

M. Mcluhan (cited in Ferguson: 1975) identified a relation between the means of communication and that which is communicated. The Television is not and can not be appropriately used as a substitute for print. It has its own rationale and presents its material in its own ways. Mcluhan rejects the belief that the printed word is outmoded.

In spite of this vast technological exploration, print continues to reign supreme. For the distance mode of education especially, it takes different forms. First, there are the course materials which at times make use of visuals. Though primarily illustrative, it also serves to ease the process of learning. But the most exciting thing, has been the personalization of written material. Devices like the student stopper and the self-assessment tests not just check the information gathered but ensure application of critical judgment. There is no absolute right and wrong. The nature of the mode does not allow for such judgments, especially where subjective interpretations are involved. The answer given would more likely be termed specimen answers followed by a kind of discussion on the comments written by the tutor. Thus the attempt is to strike a dialogue between the reader and the writer, a kind of tutorial in print, not a take it or leave it textbook. This kind of subtle persuasion, which is an attempt to involve the learner's interest, while trying to make allowance for his point of view is also an example of democratization as it operates in the distant forms. This flexibility allows the system to rid itself of the value laden criticism and comment that most often colour the classroom lectures.

Overcoming the Subjective Bias

The materials so tediously prepared have to be scrutinized by a team of experts in one's own field, related field, as also the educational technologist and the varied skills of the media team. What is at stake in such scrutiny is not one's expertise (as it was once thought in specialized areas of discipline which were safeguarded from intrusion) but the comprehensibility to a varied audience that constitute the student power. This process of criticism can be said to be one of the systems greatest strengths. Another way to overcome the subjective bias is to resort to outside help for written materials as also to constantly negotiate with other universities, in an attempt at self-examination through external criticism. However, this makes for difficulties, especially where such outside help is ignorant of the distant modes and techniques of presentation.

Supplementary Reading

Over and above such attempts to re-examine and reaffirm the distant mode of functioning a very positive step taken to keep out the structural rigidities of the curriculum is to introduce supplementary reading. Considerable care is taken to see that such reading is not used as a substitute for broadcasts or vice-versa.

The books are specially prepared for the students keeping in mind the fact that they do not have recourse to extensive library facilities that traditional universities can offer. Apart from that, background reading is also recommended in the hope that the student may at a time suitable for him, have the inclination to read what very obviously will enrich his repertoire of learning.

The Study Centres and the Summer School

In the effort to expose students to extensive reading the study centre provides the necessary help. The study-centres are an important ingredient of this system. The study centre offers 4 main facilities:

(1) It gives them an opportunity to get together with other students. (2) It is a move towards co-operative education, instead of the competition that is encouraged in traditional institutions. (3) It also provides for seeing and hearing programmes together and gives the right incentive for discussion.

(4) The study center also offers opportunity for consultation with a counsellor.

The Summer school, however, provides a chance for real university experience, though it was also conceived as partly a remedial kind of a programme.

Tutor Comment and Evaluation

The basic help is given by the tutor through the correspondence tuition. This is the most difficult part of the programme, in the British Open University, more so, if the discipline is interdisciplinary and calls for the co-ordination of two or three members from different faculties. Tutor comments are specially significant and are considerably effective when there is a correlation between the marginal comment and the personal note.

A system of continuous examination and evaluation eases the tension by its innovatory move to take the best two thirds of work into consideration. However the continuous assessment and the final examination is ridden with problems. For while the Computer Marked Assignments are easy in assessing the science subjects, in humanities, one is not so sure if one can draw too rigid a line between factual knowledge and critical judgment.

The Dilemma of Individualizing and Standardizing

Catering as it does to the working adult, the Distance systems as we have seen, has to be more and more flexible. As a system that enables the adult to go about his work as he educates himself, it has necessarily had to relax its organization structurally as well as in functional terms. While the structural flexibility is obvious especially in the face of the rigidities of the traditional educational systems, the functional aspect has remained of some controversy. This has to do both with its drive to meet the mass educational purpose, while at the same time make it individualized. In so far as the Distance System has pledged to compensate for the lacks in the traditional educational system, it must be itself accessible to a large population with educational potential, that has been ignored by the traditional educational set up. To create opportunity for this vast reservoir of resources the Distance education mode has made extensive use of the industrialized procedures. As Peters puts it, Distance Education can be seen as a parallel development to industrialization. It makes use of rationalized procedures to invoke *those feelings of conflict* suppressed by the traditional school curricula. Therefore there is an inherent paradox in arousing content through a method that has been traditionally considered repressive, namely the industrial procedures.

Autonomy

At the learner's end, individualization or autonomy is one would think naturally available as the learner is an independent working adult. The implications for *Androgogy* are obvious. An attempt to draw on the learner's experience is part of the distant modes way of the educating the adult into self-awareness. As was stated earlier, by Gelpi, both the content and the form must be amenable to the adult learner.

Account has to be taken of what Holec (1985) observes as the ability to function autonomously. This, says Holec should not be confused with the desirability to do so. The ability to function autonomously includes decisions regarding setting objectives, pacing and even evaluating one's progress. Therefore, it is important to discriminate between one who is ready to struggle on one's own self and others who do not possess the necessary tools to do so.

Control

However, to be relevant to the educational philosophy, the autonomy has to be offset by a relevant control (Garrison:

1989). Or else, the teaching-learning experience would make no sense. Distance modes are no different in this sense. Guidance is essential. As Allwright (1982) earlier observed, guidance is imperative in so far as it helps the learner perceive his needs. Dickinson (1987) similarly talks about self-direction being a notional scale, with lesser or greater degrees of self-direction ultimately leading towards autonomy. Moore (1983) refers to this as a dialogue between the structured and the unstructured material. With respect to language teaching and learning, this is very significant. The context of language learning is both context-tied and context-free in so far as it is both a product of society and yet flexible enough to imply meanings beyond it. Conceptually then, English language teaching through the Distance Mode takes advantage of this duality, as it fluctuates between individualization and standardization. Language teaching and learning, as the distance mode realizes it, is a collaborative experience, through acts of communication. And communication necessarily has to be two ways, for it to be meaningful. It is in this context that *control* becomes meaningful, as the teacher and the learner operate within the educational framework.

Teacher/Learner Relationship

The structural flexibility of the Distance Systems are also obvious in the authority relations between teacher and student. The counsellors as also the counselling sessions are co-operative ventures where the individual is free to express himself and his opinions. More often the counsellor's job as some one points out is "to make coffee and offer suggestions" which is a total deviation from the traditional role of the teacher. Of crucial importance is the fact that the counsellor is often a morale booster in so far as he has to provide encouragement and suggestions in times where motivation is failing, a familiar incidence in the distant mode.

Language Curriculum

Within the language curriculum itself, this flexibility of the Open University makes sense in the range of learning tasks that will have to be presented both in terms of linguistic and cognitive complexity. Linguistic complexity is implied more in the form of grammatical instruction, while cognitive complexity may call for a kind of rational thinking pertaining to the task at hand. However, this rational thinking is not based on the Piagetion assumption of the ideal learner. It accommodates a range of perspectives, depending on the social set up to which the student belongs. Yet, it is not limiting in the sense that it explores and even asserts the possibility of multiple perspectives. This flexibility in content is especially liberating for those adults who have had to function within the narrow frames of lower stream education. It helps to understand that other socializations and meanings are possible and with effort, attainable, provided even the power relations are flexible.

Process Redefined

This structural flexibility of the Distance Systems then also allow for a functional flexibility that to a large extent lets the learner decide on his priorities by making him aware of them. The process elements that were held in high esteem seem to make more sense in the context of the Distance Mode, than in the traditional educational systems. For, unlike the Progressive endeavour to seek universal solutions in a social vaccum, the open systems in the distance mode struggle to achieve the potential possibilities within a given social setting. This social definition is however not limiting. The Distance Mode's, attempt to educate makes for an 'awareness' that moves beyond this limiting framework of given social definitions and allow for other interpretations arising from similar other social constructs. As it does so, it questions why certain other possibilities cannot be captured, given a definite social cast. Through this questioning it allows for a restructuring, a resocialisation, by reminding us that every social setting is a human construct; its rigidity is only a mask, which can be broken and remoulded for a different purpose. All this is possible provided one is given the political power to do so.

The Opportunity to Resocialize

The Distance Mode exposes, as it were, the socialization patterns and legitimations for what they are; in other words, it exposes the human complexity that designed these patterns. And in so doing, it allows its pupils the opportunity to resocialize. When socializations are human handiworks one is as good as the other. There is therefore the insight that with effort, one has a range of patterns from which to choose. Precisely in giving this choice, the distance mode operates in the true democratic spirit. Yet, since socialization itself is a kind of habitualization and habits die hard, the distant mode does not offer this choice on a platter. A lot of effort is called for before the individual can realize that he can make a choice. In this sense the Distance Mode ideally speaking, refuses to acknowledge the hierarchies in the division of labour. The different divisions are simply differently designated works, which carry no label of the top or bottom level.

In the Process curriculum of the Progressivists there is no guarantee that the elements of democracy, the inter-disciplinary nature of the subjects and so on, are not in themselves structured in so far as they are well within the classroom bounds and within the power of the teacher. Griffin (1983) says that the traditional set up puts the teacher in a repressive role. The rigidity of the structures and the evaluation systems, do not allow for *genuine choice* to operate despite organizational looseness. The apparent looseness tightens the divisional structures even more strongly and it seems as if the pupil is alienated as much from the school as from his home. If the traditional structures were transparent, despite the rigidity, the democratization of the Process curriculum render it even more opaque to anyone, outside the belief-system. Bernstein (1975) describes these changes as a change from visible to invisible pedagogies. *Process* set ups here become institutionalized in the sense that any one who doesn't believe in it have no place in it. A legitimating process that includes pupils, and teachers is set in motion so that the illusion of democratic choices is set up. In this set up while locating errors becomes easy, locating the responsibility becomes comparatively difficult. Failures, which earlier could be identified with the class outcomes become individualized, especially for the working class pupils. Social gifts as Bourdieu (1974) states are naturalized.

A Summing Up

Justifiably then for 'Process" to be realized to its fullest extent, the rigidity of the structures, as also the curriculum content should be made flexible. Given the working adult in the distant mode, process naturally yields itself to unveil the patterns of socializations and allows for a reformulation. The inter-disciplinary approach makes better sense to the adult than to the younger child as also the immediate relevance of the subject to his particular socio-economic reality. These dimensions are beyond the school student who is forced to accommodate himself to a homogeneous set up as the school.

To the adult, however, the Distant system offers definite advantages. For instance the constant interaction with other universities provides further impetus for the democratization processes. The Open mode has a transparency from which students outside the system can also benefit. While 'Process' curriculum as it operates in traditional systems remains untested and seldom criticized, in the distance mode, it is subjected to severe scrutiny. It is finally this criticism that makes it's processes more genuine, more trustworthy.

Yet the Distance Mode is not a revolutionary break. It has emerged from within the framework of traditional education. Perhaps this is the reason why it has to be judged against the perspective of the traditional educational set up. The criticism that it favours middle classes, despite its claims is not unwarranted, considering its assumptions regarding not merely literacy but also the continual experience of reading and writing. If it continues to attract those who already have had some taste of education, then new means for motivation will have to be found. Similar feelings are reiterated by Willem van der Eyken (1974) when he says that outside the political rhetoric the distance systems have failed to attract the exhausted manual labour. They have, he asserts, only pulled the white collared into their realms.

Implications for the Language Curriculum

In thus widening the scope, the Open University, it seems, has opened almost all possible channels for encouraging language development. Not simply through print, but through T.V. and Broadcasting, language learning becomes a motivating factor in itself. The flexibility both at the level of conception and in terms of curriculum development, should alley all doubts about language learning through the Distance Mode.

In terms of specific contribution to the development of the language curriculum, the Distance Mode, as has already been pointed out, makes for a dynamism. This dynamic quality emerges from the credibility that the Distance Mode gives to the social context of the learner, the opinion the learner has of learning and the methods suitable for the learner. Given the status of English language learning in India, the Distance Mode, has to take account of the purposes for which English is learnt, the learner's native language competence and the particular variety of English that can result from efforts to translate. Similarly, curriculum features that include spoken English should broaden to permit regional accents, without undue stress on the learner. Given the second language status, English language teaching cannot project any particular model. In particular, since the most crucial aspects of learning takes place through interaction with the materials, these have to be dealt with utmost care.

Whether the objective is to teach the basic skills, or help students get an idea of the learning strategies considerable options must be given in the material. Further, since the purpose of English in India is more utilitarian, the focus, will be more on language as medium, as a vehicle to communicate rather than on the study of the language itself, for its linguistic features and so on. Language curriculum as developed though the distance mode would, atleast in theory, seem to suggest a deviation from the language curriculum of the traditional syllabus. Yet this not limit distance education from exploiting English as a language in itself. It has already been observed that a purely functional perception is limiting. The attempt to draw on Experiential knowledge should allow for a richer basis for language teaching and learning.

What the Open University does is to bring out the challenges before the public gaze. The facts can no longer be hidden behind a smokescreen of documents and reports. We have to choose between selective higher education and mass higher education. If the selective system is retained, one has to justify that decision with a great deal more conviction than is at present the case, and in the background the Open University will forever be disproving the fact. But if we go for the Open University then the entire infrastructure of the traditional systems would be threatened.

Conclusion

Thus the Distance Mode can very definitely be cast as an alternate form of curriculum organization. It's openness and transparencies challenge the traditional systems and provoke them. So in a way, the very existence of the Distance Mode can bring about more refinements into the traditional curricula. Infact a deeper probing could unveil possibilities for recycling some of the insights gained through the Distance Mode of functioning, into the traditional systems. Despite the realizable objectives of the Distance Mode, it has become customary to approach it in a rather apologetic fashion. This is something one has to critically re-examine. The Distance Mode should not be seen as an apology for the traditional systems, if one intends to benefit from it; rather it is education from a different perspective, more accessible, more open, and therefore more trust-worthy.

7

Conclusion

A Note of Caution

Through these Chapters, an attempt has been made to discuss the possibilities of the Distance Mode as an alternate form of the curriculum. As we have seen, the democratic processes of education, that the traditional educational systems aim at are best achieved through the Distance Mode. Of crucial importance has been the language teaching and learning programme through the Distance Mode.

If second language learning and teaching has any similarity to the first language learning as the SLA research struggles to announce, it is best achieved through the self pacing, self education schemes of the Distance Mode. This is significant as the learner here is an adult with sufficient competence in the native language. So linguistic capability is something that one has to take for granted. But the kind of language he is exposed to depends on the social set up in which he lives and also the kind of occupation he is involved in. Account has to be taken of these factors, in considering language acquisition.

In so far as English is a second language and is used for a limited number of hours, the teachers or the learners cannot be forced to acquire standard models of English. In fact, this becomes impossible, if one views language as a dynamic that is vitalized in various other language environments. English is no exception. In so far as we recognize this, English has to be recognized with all its regional flavour, provided communication is not affected. An initial functional perception in terms of needs, however has to be broadened as English should be learned for its status as language. This is specially important in so far as it is required in the higher levels of education.

However such a flexible framework is eternally threatened by the danger of the system becoming centrifugal. The threat is not so much from the traditional set up as from its own formulation. That the Distance Systems have attracted a large number of white collar workers and have not succeeded in attracting labour, is now generally acknowledged. Although attempts are on to reach this particular section of society, the temptation to collapse into yet other form of traditional authoritative structure is not far. An educated working class in full possession of a national tradition, says Birnbaum (1974) awaits a much fuller development of projects like the open University.

Speaking not a little skeptically, Birnbaum observes, that the belief in the socialist mission of the University will not essentially alter the relations of property and power. There is, according to him, a special appeal for the technocrat in the economy the project offers. That the Open University offers a second chance should not blind us, he says, to the technocratic imperatives at work: the availability of social investment for this purpose is connected with the changing composition of the labour force, the increase in its educational attainments made necessary by technological development. It is, he observes, the capacity to understand the social uses of technology that alone can enable contemporary population to withstand a servitude to technocratic rulers.

Birnbaum also hints at the danger of Open University's technical utilization of the means of mass culture for the transmission of high culture. The Open University experiment he warns, may form a new generation of academics able to use a few wider range of concepts and method capable of relating knowledge to the aims of inquiry rather than to the rigidities of fixed disciplines. Most interdisciplinary routines have, he warns us, become centrifugal; the claims of the discipline reassert themselves. The tendency he fears, is clearly not absent at the Open University: it ought to be resisted. Distance systems, it has been said, are precisely in this danger of doing what Birnbaum describes as *going centrifugal*. Not merely by subjects but by suppressing conflict feelings in the masses it can become centrifugal in yet another dangerous way. It can alienate a complete section of the public to give in to the powerful few. If the South African experience, where the Distance Systems have managed to keep out a vast populace from interferring with the Racist policies, is anything to go by, then Distance would seem to be even more authoritative than it appears. On the other hand, if it has the potential to alienate an entire community, it also has the potential to wake another into a revolution. It is with these positive notes that one should think of the Distance Mode of Education.

Bibliography

Allman Paula, 1983, 'The Nature and Process of Adult Development'. in Tight (e.d.) 1983.

Allwright, Dick, 1982a, 'Perceiving and Pursuing Learner Needs'. in Geddes and Sturtridge (eds.)

Allwright, Dick, 1984, 'The Importance of Interaction in Classroom Language Learning'. in *Applied Linguistics* 5/2 1984.

Allwright, Dick, 1980, 'Turns, Topics and Tasks'. in Larsen Freeman (ed.)

Apple, Michael, 1979, *Ideology and the Curriculum.* London: Routledge and Kegan Paul.

Apple, Michael, 1980, 'Curricular Form and the Logic of Technical Control'. in Walker et al (eds.) 1980.

Baath, John A., 1983, 'Theoretical Models for Planning Correspondence Courses'. in *Epistolodiactica* 1983.

Bantock, G.H., 1975, 'Towards a Theory of Popular Education'. in Goldby et al (eds.) 1975.

Berger, Peter and Luckmann, Thomas, 1967, *The Social Construction of Reality.* New York: Anchor Books.

Bernstein, Basil, 1975, *Class, Codes and Control*, Volume 3, London: Routledge and Kegan Paul.

Bourdieu, Pierre, 1974, 'The School as a Conservative Force'. translated J.C. Whitehouse in Eggleston (ed.) 1974.

Bowles, Samuel and Gintis, Herbert, 1980, 'Contradiction and Reproduction in Educational Theory'. in Walker et. al (eds.) 1980.

Breen, M.P., 1987, 'Contemporary Paradigms in Syllabus Design'. Part I & II in *Language Teaching* 20/34.

Breen, M.P. and Candlin, C.N., 1980, 'The Essentials of a Communicative Curriculum in Language Teaching'. in *Applied Linguistics.* 1/2.

Brumfit, C.J. (ed.), 1985, *General English Syllabus Design.* ELTDocs. 118. Oxford: Pergamon.

Bruner, Jerome, S., 1971, *Relevance of Education.* New York: W.W. Norton and Company.

Bruner, Jerome. S., 1969, *The Process of Education.* Cambridge: Harvard University.

Bruner, Jerome. S., 1975, 'Language as an Instrument of Thought'. in A Davies (ed.) 1975.

Campbell, Sarah (ed.), 1976, *Piaget Sampler.* New York: John Wiley & Sons Inc.

Chia, Noel, 1993, 'In Search of a Curriculum for Distance Learning'. in *Epistolodidactica* 1993.

Candlin, C.N., 1985, 'Syllabus Design as a Critical Process'. in C.J. Brumfit (ed.) 1985.

Clarke, J.L., 1987, *Curriculum Renewal in Language Learning.* Oxford: O.U.P.

Coldeway Don. O., 1982, 'What does Educational Psychology tell us about Adult Learner at a Distance?'. in Daniel S. John et al (ed.) 1982.

Cummins, Jim and Swain, Merril, 1986, *Bilingualism in Education: Aspects of Theory, Research and Practice.* New York: Longman.

Daniel S. John. et. al (ed.), 1982, *Learning at a Distance: A World Perspective.* Edmonton: Athabersca University ICCE.

Davies, Alan (ed.), 1975, *Problems of Language and Learning.* London: Heinemann.

Dewey, Jonh, 1916, *Democracy and Education.* New York: The Macmillan Co.

Dewey, John, 1975, 'The Child and the Curriculum'. in Goldby et. al (eds.) 1975.

Dickinson, Leslie, 1987, *Self Instruction in Language Learning.* Cambridge: Cambridge University Press.

Durkheim, Emile, 1956, *Education and Sociology.* translated Sherwood. D. Fox. New York: The Free Press.

Eggleston, John, 1974, *Contemporary Research in the Sociology of Education.* London: Methuen.

Eggleston, John, 1977, *The Sociology of the School Curriculum.* London: Routledge and Kegan Paul.

Entwistle, Herald, 1978, *Class, Culture and Education.* London: Methuen.

Eyken, Willem van der, 1974, 'The Seeds of Radical Change'. in Tunstall (ed.) 1974.

Freeman, Larsen Diane (ed.), 1980, *Discourse Analysis in Second Language Research.* Rowley Mass: NewBury.

Ferguson, John (ed.), 1975, *The Open University from within.* London: University of London Press.

Freire, Paulo, 1983, *The Pedagogy of the Oppresses*, translated. Myra Bergman. Ramos: Penguin

Garrison, D.R., 1989, *Understanding Distance Education: A Framework for the Future.* London: Routledge.

Geddes, Marion and Sturtridge, Gill,1982, *Individualisation*: London: Modern English Publishers.

Goldby et al (eds.), 1975, *Curriculum Design.* London: Open University Press.

Grice, Paul, 1989, *Studies in the Way of Words.* Cambridge: Havard University Press.

Griffin, Colin, 1983, *Adult and Lifelong Education.* London and Canberra: Croom Helm.

Hirst, Paul. H., 1975, 'Logic and the Curriculum'. in Goldby et al (eds.) 1975.

Holec, Henri., 1985, 'On autonomy: Some elementary concepts'. in Riley (ed.) 1985.

Ignacy, Waneineicez, 1982, 'The Adult Learners: Who are

they? Why and Where do they learn?'. Daniel. S. John (ed.). 1982.

Knowles, Malcolm, 1983, 'Androgogy: an emerging technology in Adult Learning'. in Tight. M. (ed.). 1983.

Krashen, Stephen, 1961, *Second Language Acquisition and Second Language Learning*. Oxford: Pergamon.

Krashen, Stephen, 1985, *Input Hypothesis*. London: Longman.

Lynch, Kathleen, 1989, *The Hidden Curriculum*. London: The Falmer Press.

Moore, Michael, 1983, 'On a Theory of Independent Study'. in Sewart et al (eds.) 1983.

Peters, Otto, 1983, 'Distance Teaching and Industrial Production for Comparative interpretation: an outline'. in Sewart et. al. (eds.) 1983.

Ramphal, Anita, 1992, 'A Possible Orality for Science'. *Interchange* Vol. 23/2 pp. 227-244.

Riley, Phillip (ed.), 1985, *Discourse and Learning*. London: Longman.

Tunstall, Jeremy (ed.), 1974, *The Open · University Opens*. London: Routledge and Kegan Paul Ltd.

Sewart, David et al (eds.), 1983, *Distance Education: International Perspectives*. London: Croom Helm.

Tight, Malcolm (ed.), 1983, 'Education for Adults' in *Adult Learning and Education*. London: Croom Helm in association with the OU. Vol. 1.

Vygotsky, L., 1986, *Thought and Langauge*. Cambridge: The MIT Press.

Walker et al (eds.), 1980, *Schooling, Ideology and Curriculum*. England: The Falmer Press.

Wedemeyer, Charles, 1983, 'The Backdoor Learning in the Learning Society'. in Sewart et al (eds.) 1983.

Index